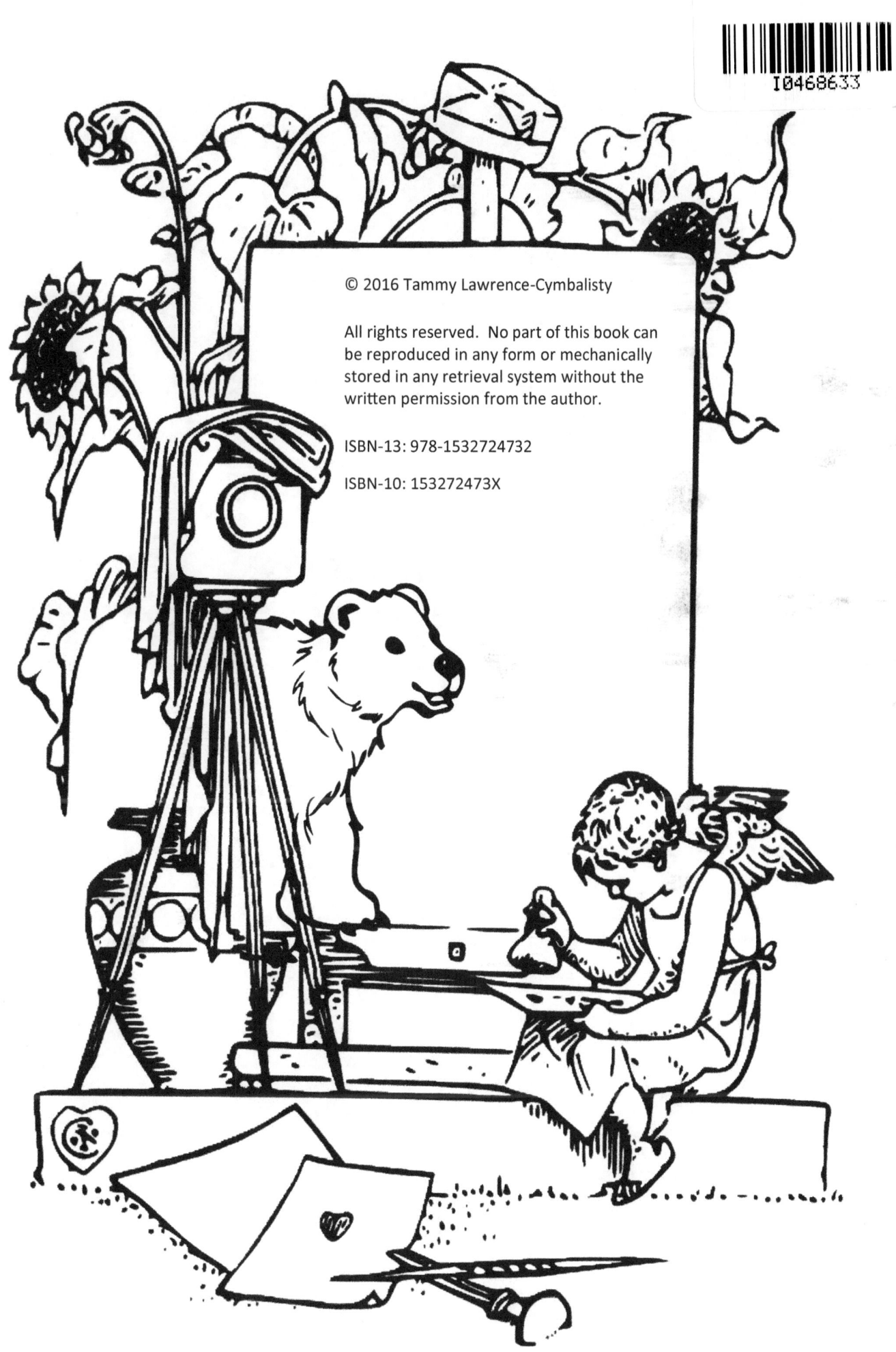

ISBN-13: 978-1532724732

ISBN-10: 153272473X

I0468633

Welcome to the My Bear Totem Colouring book! Thank you so much for your purchase.

I want to share with you what brought this series of colouring books to fruition. I was doing some research on what my next project should be and stumbled across an owl to colour (I have Owl as my totem). I thought about creating a colouring book. I asked the universe, "Should I be focusing on this?" I put the question out there, let it go and left for work. Within two blocks of the house I noticed a billboard with the words "In The Dark; an upcoming exhibit at a museum in Waterloo, Ontario. I laughed when I saw it. Staring back at me from the bulletin board were a huge set of Owl eyes! "Maybe that's a message?" I kept going on my path not giving it much more thought.

I arrived at work ten minutes later to see a tiny envelope on the floor where I normally place my yoga mat (I'm grateful to be a Yoga Teacher) with my name on the front of it. I open it up to find a tiny pewter Owl with the words "Give a Hoot" inscribed on the back! I burst out laughing and shared the story with Wendy; the woman who had gifted me. That decided it there and then!

After I completed the Owl Totem colouring book I thought why stop there? All of the animals of the Zodiac should be represented. I am surrounded by Bears in my world. I love them so much in fact I even married one!

Bears in the Native American Lore is for those born between Aug 22—Sept. 21. The Bear pays attention to detail, is filled with deep wisdom and introspection. Bear represents power, strength and healing. You can find out more about the Native American Lore by searching "Native American Zodiac signs" to see which animal you are.

Whether the Bear is your totem or you simply adore this beautiful creature I hope you enjoy it. Go grab your markers, pens, pencil crayons or paints and your creative juices!

I would suggest placing a piece of paper (you could also choose waxed paper) behind the pictures particularly if you are choosing wet mediums to prevent any bleed-through. The pictures have a page between them to help with this additionally. However if you, like me, enjoy using acrylics or watercolour you may need the additional support for the page.

You'll find lots of areas in the pictures to add additional creations. For example you could turn it into a journal by writing about your day in the blank areas, play with some interesting fonts or add your favourite affirmations. You are the artist here so whatever you create will be perfect!

Happy colouring!

Wishing you many continued blessings,

Tammy

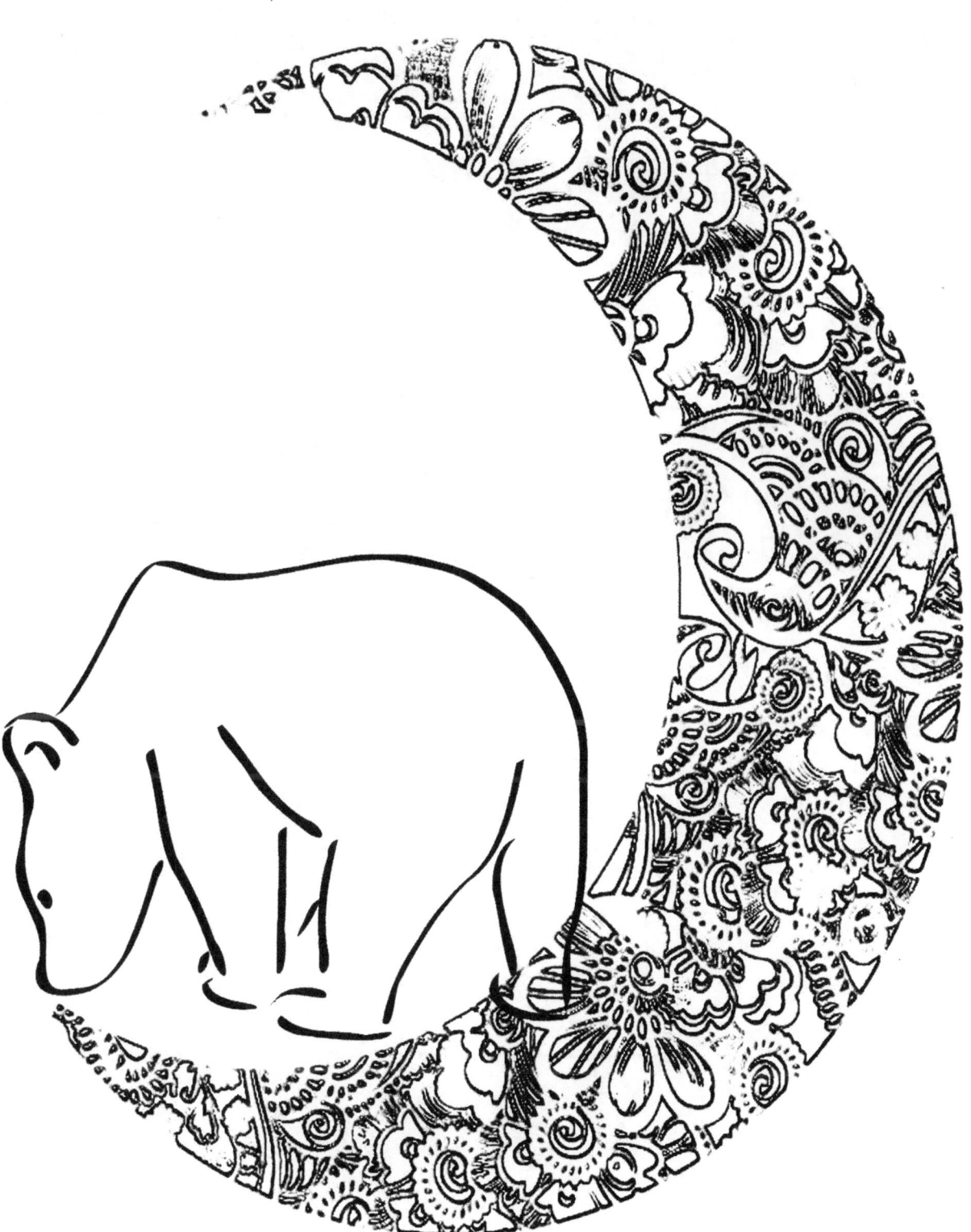

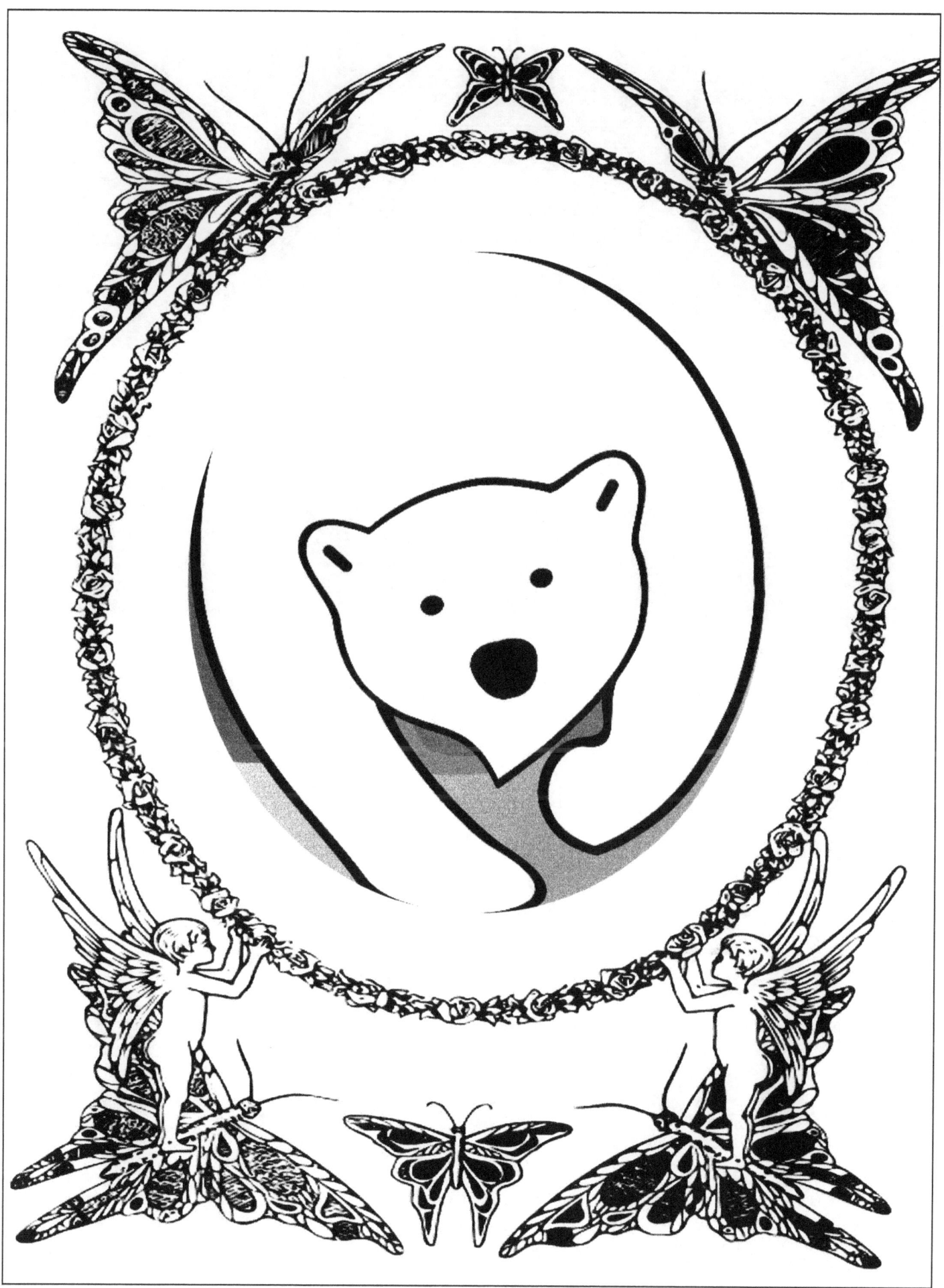

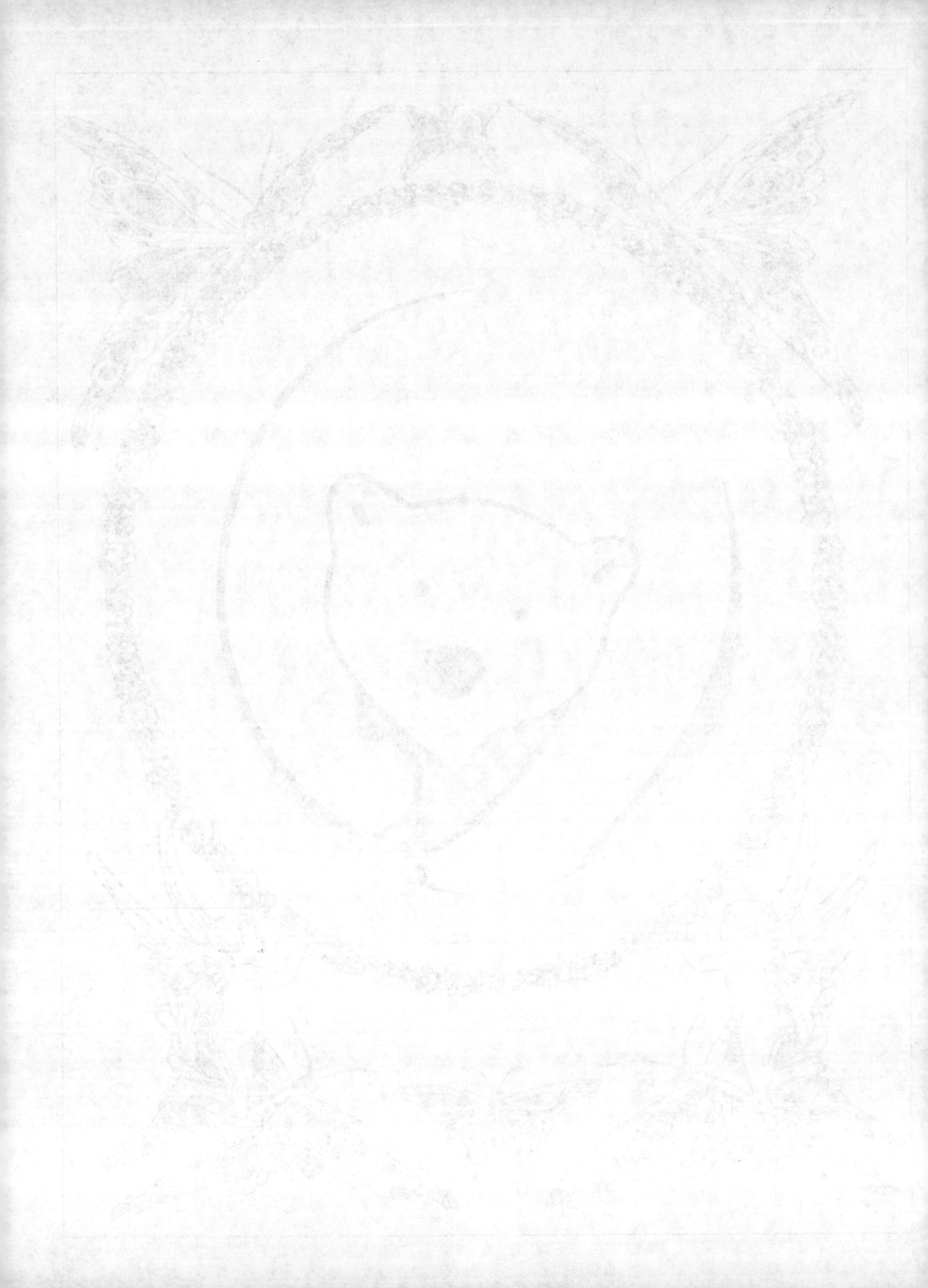

Introspection

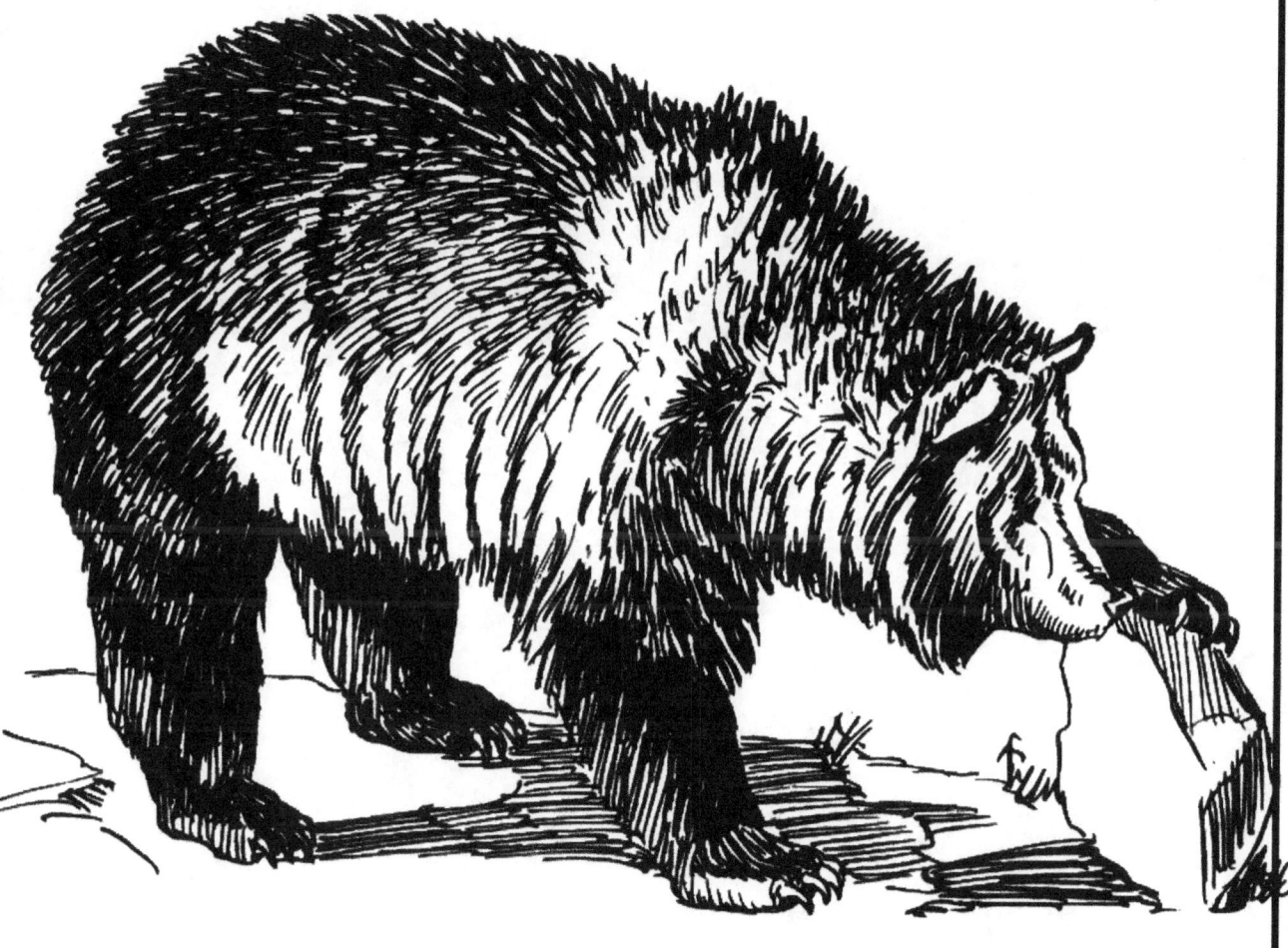

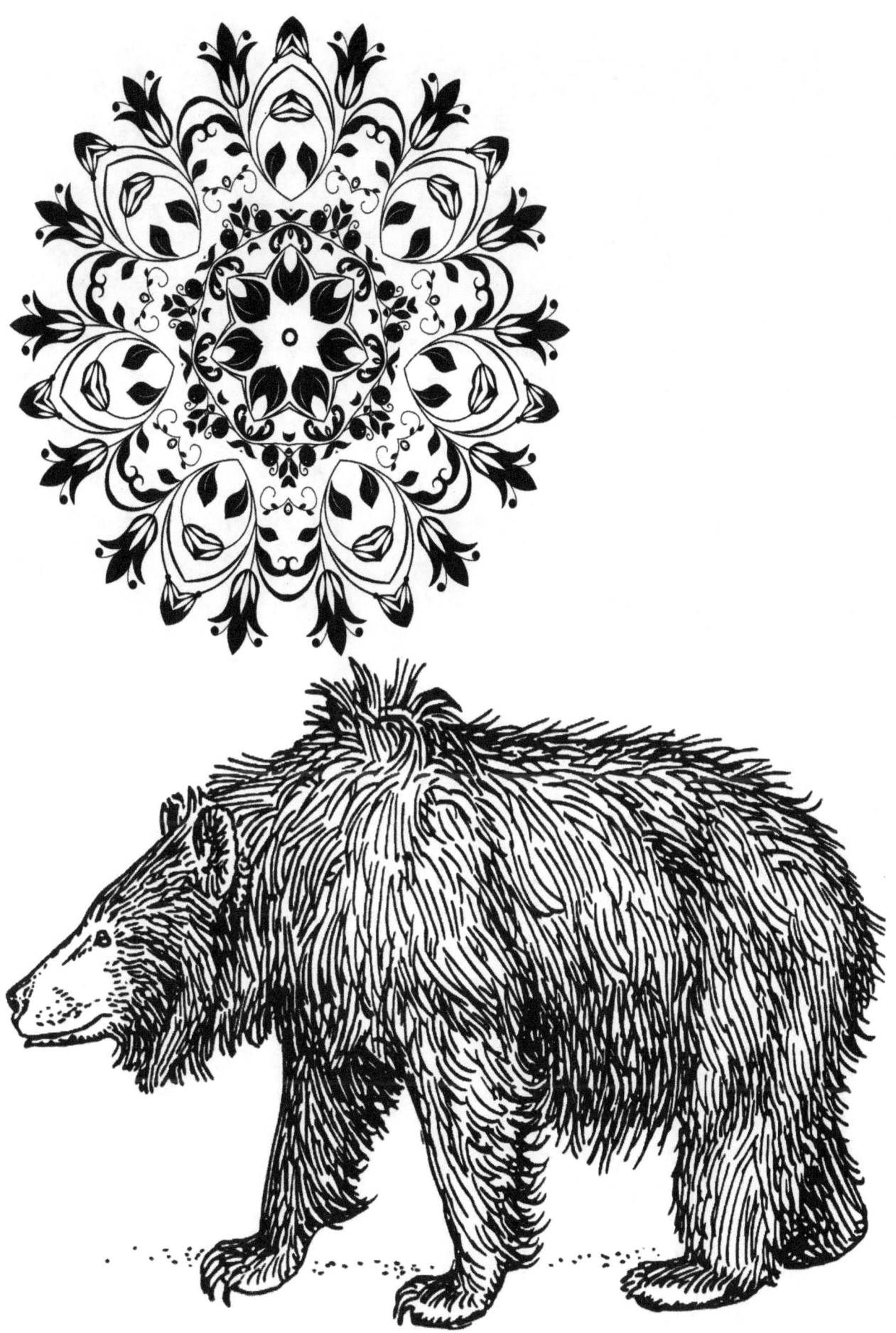

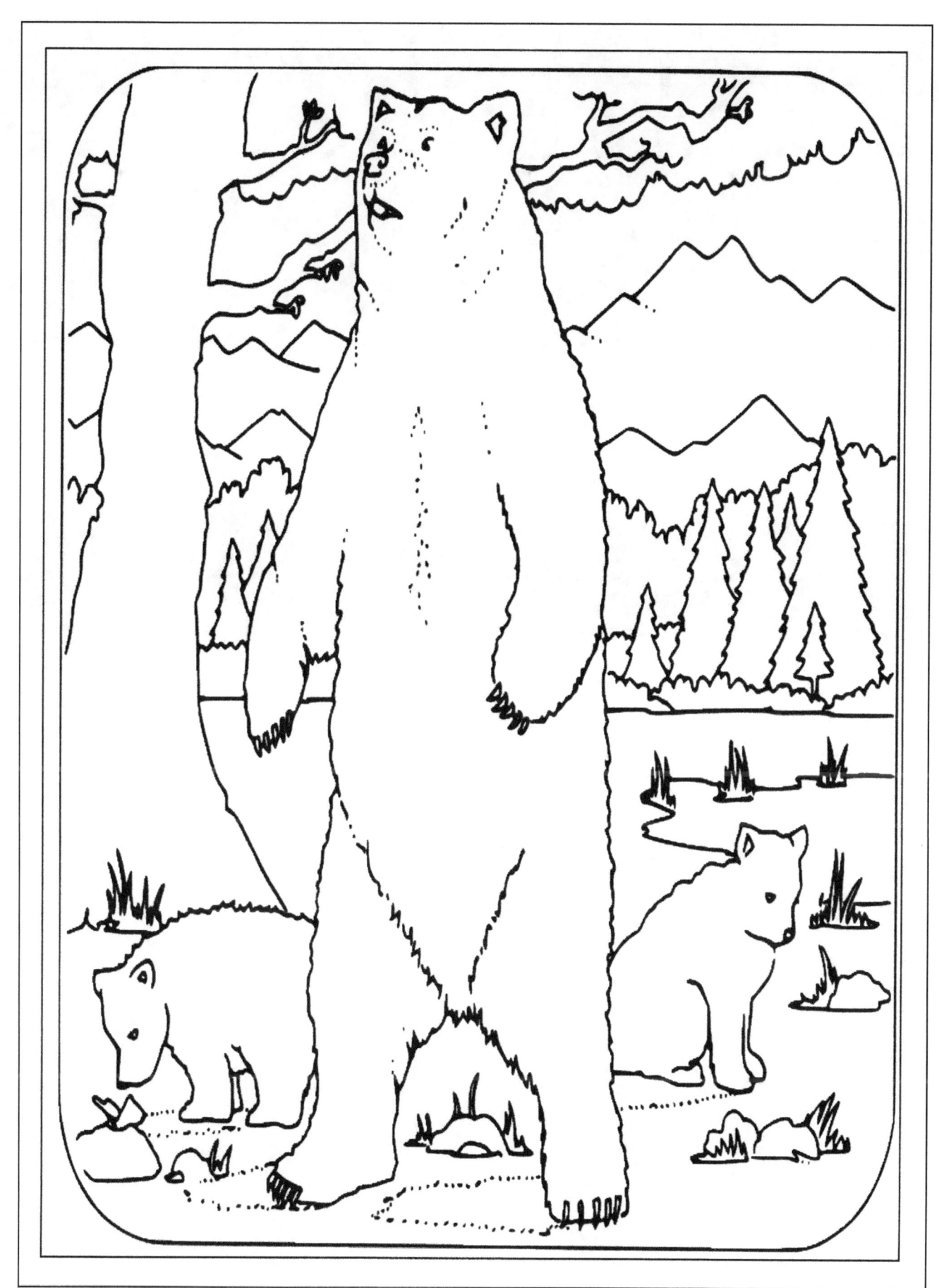

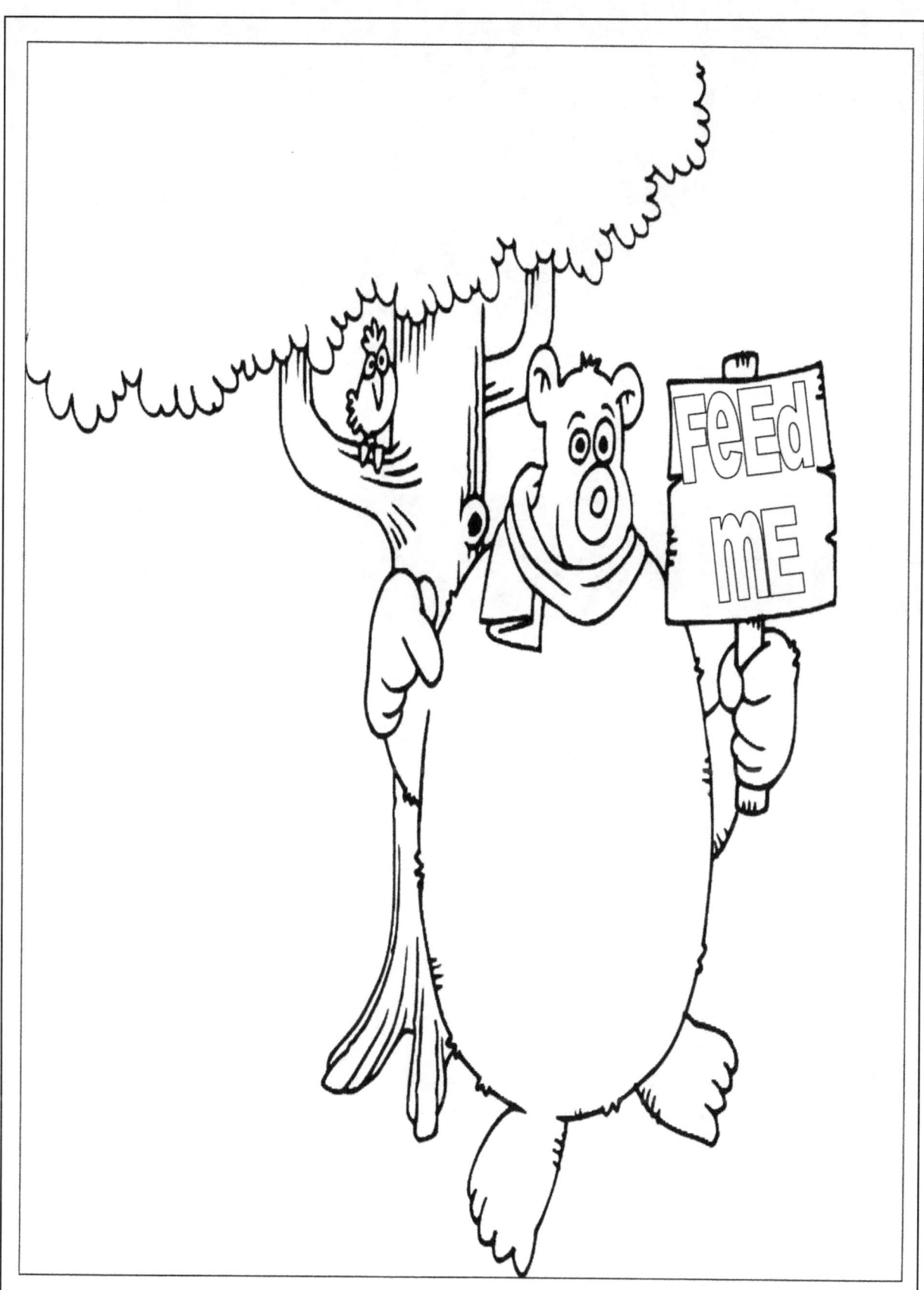

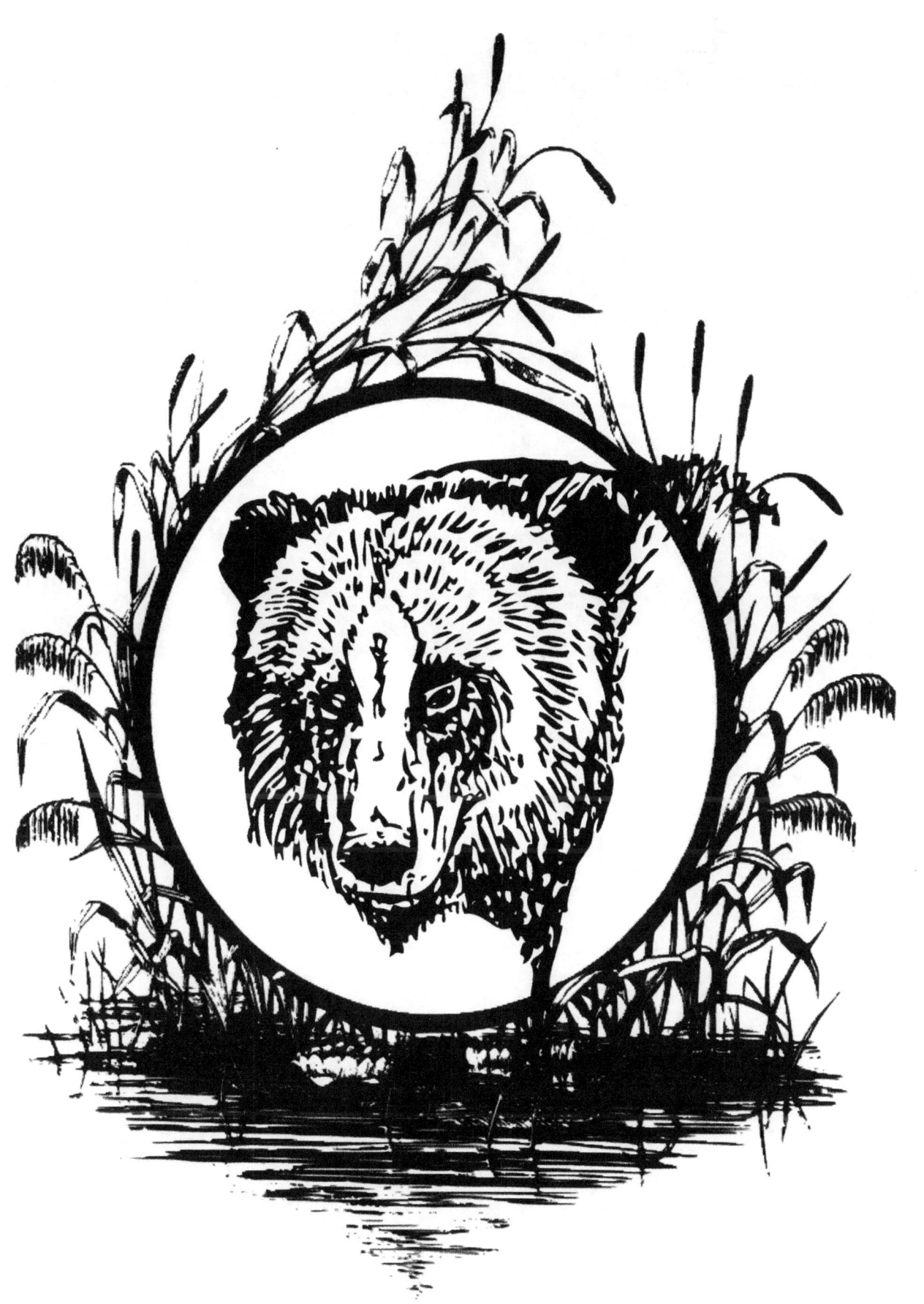

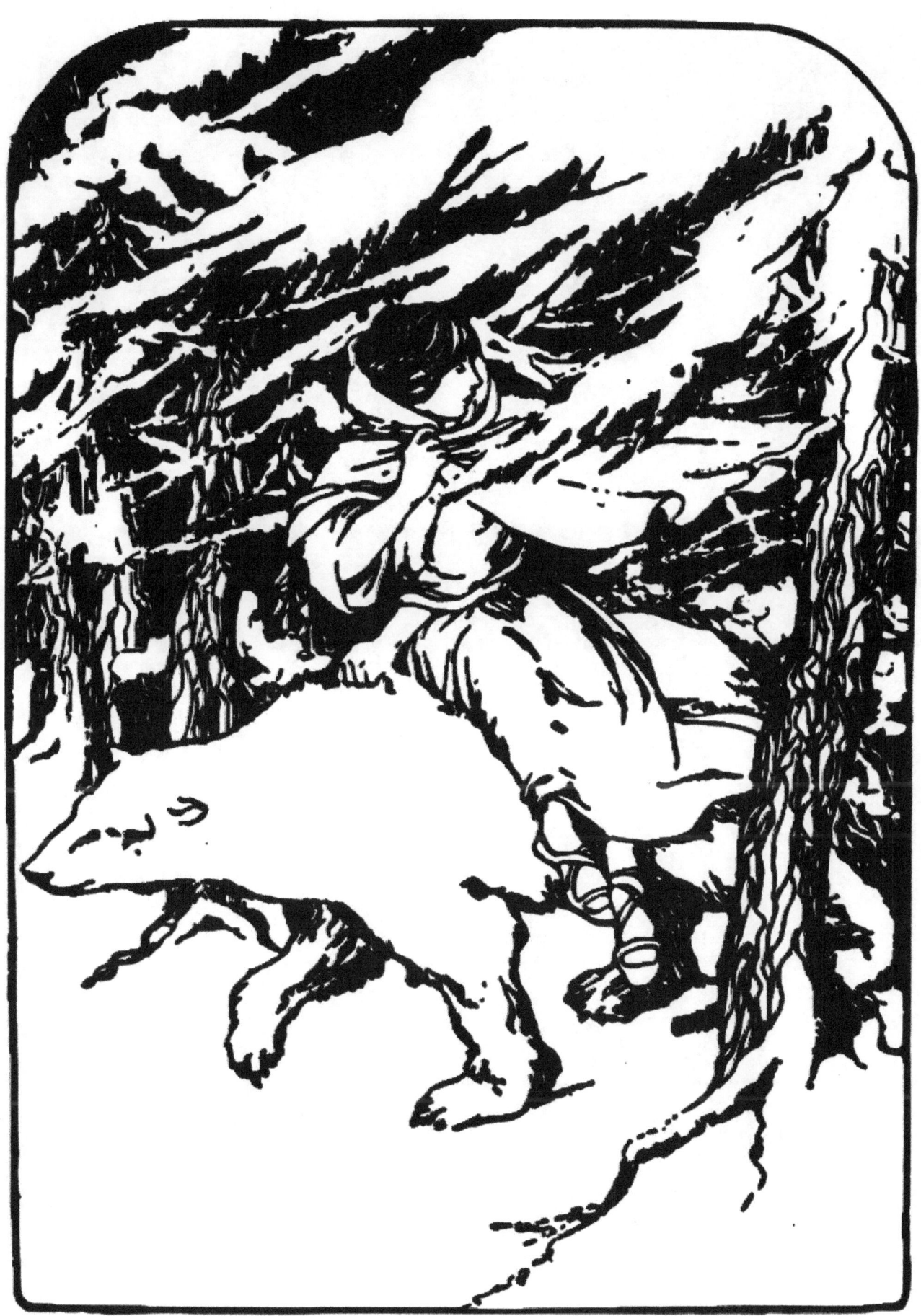

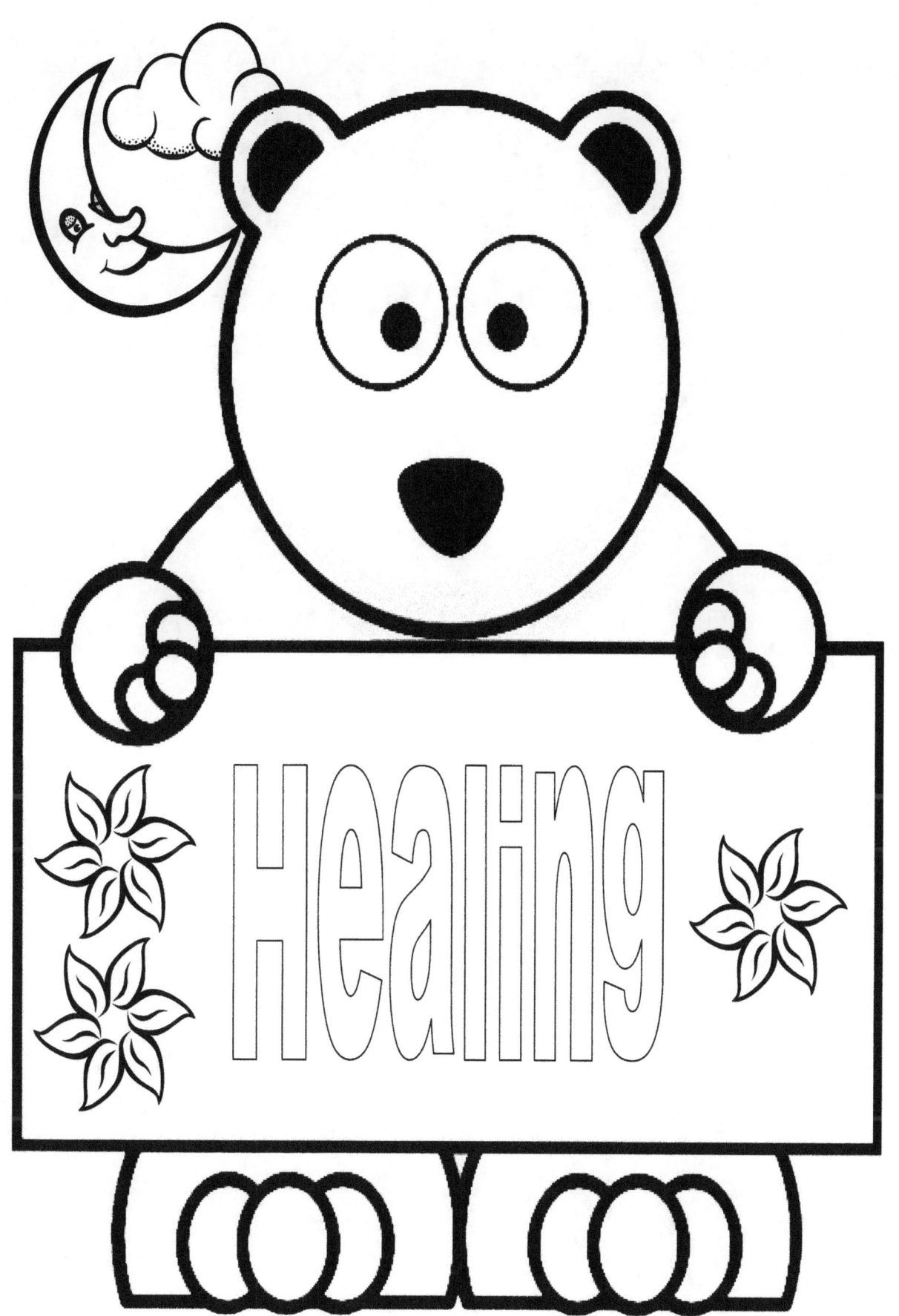

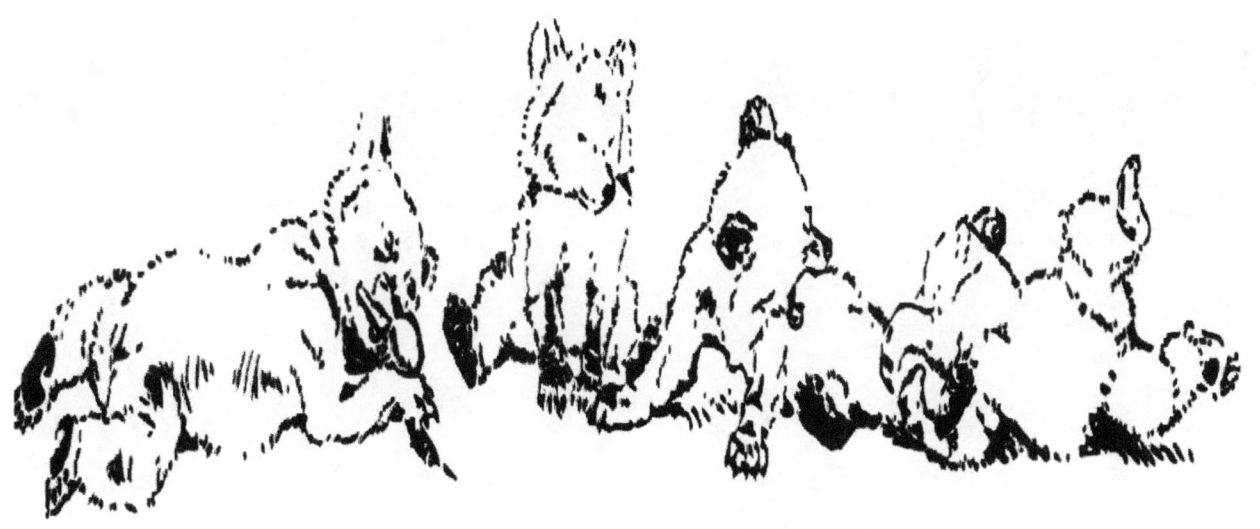

To LIVE with Gratitudes

⋙ forever

IN my

heart

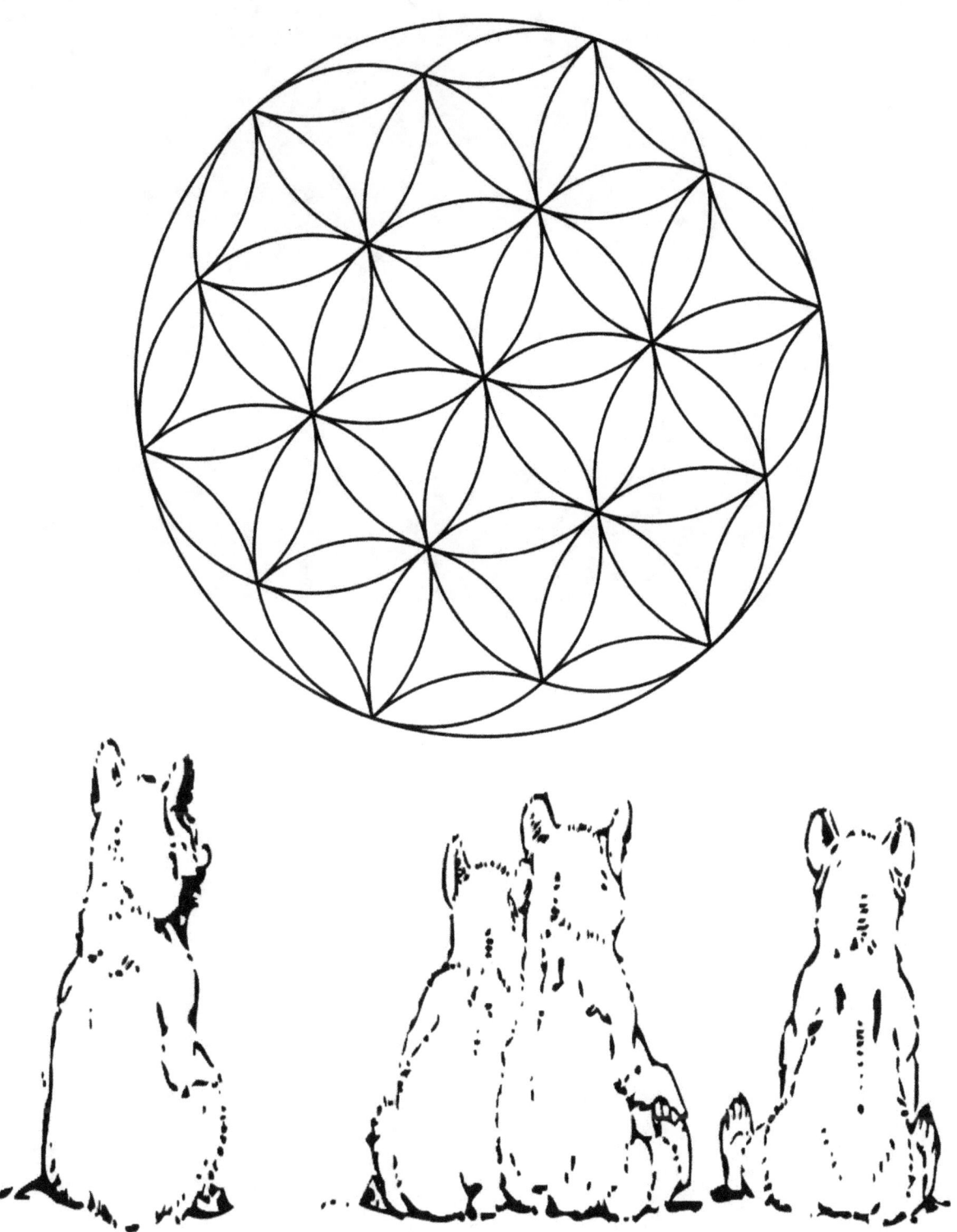

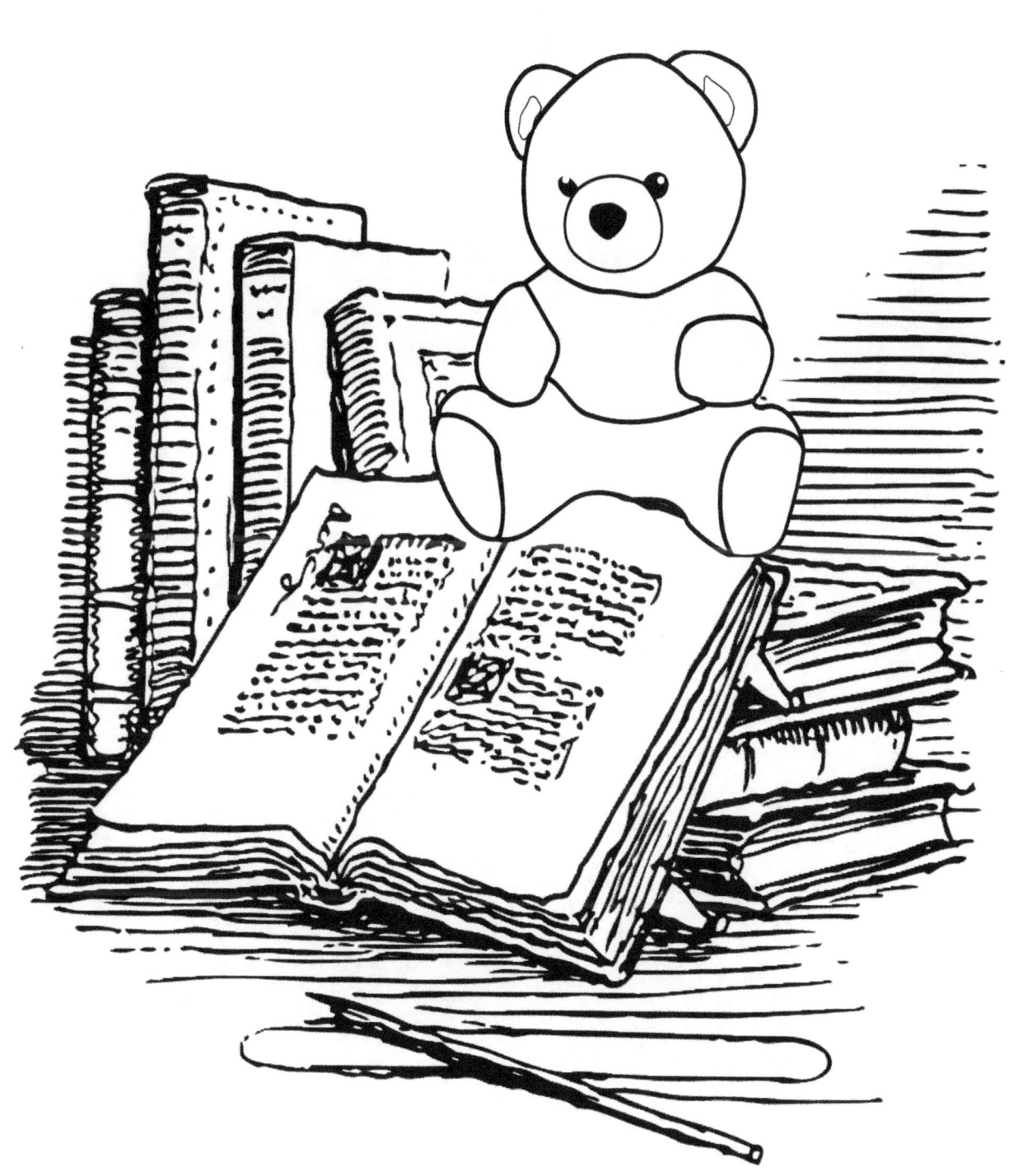

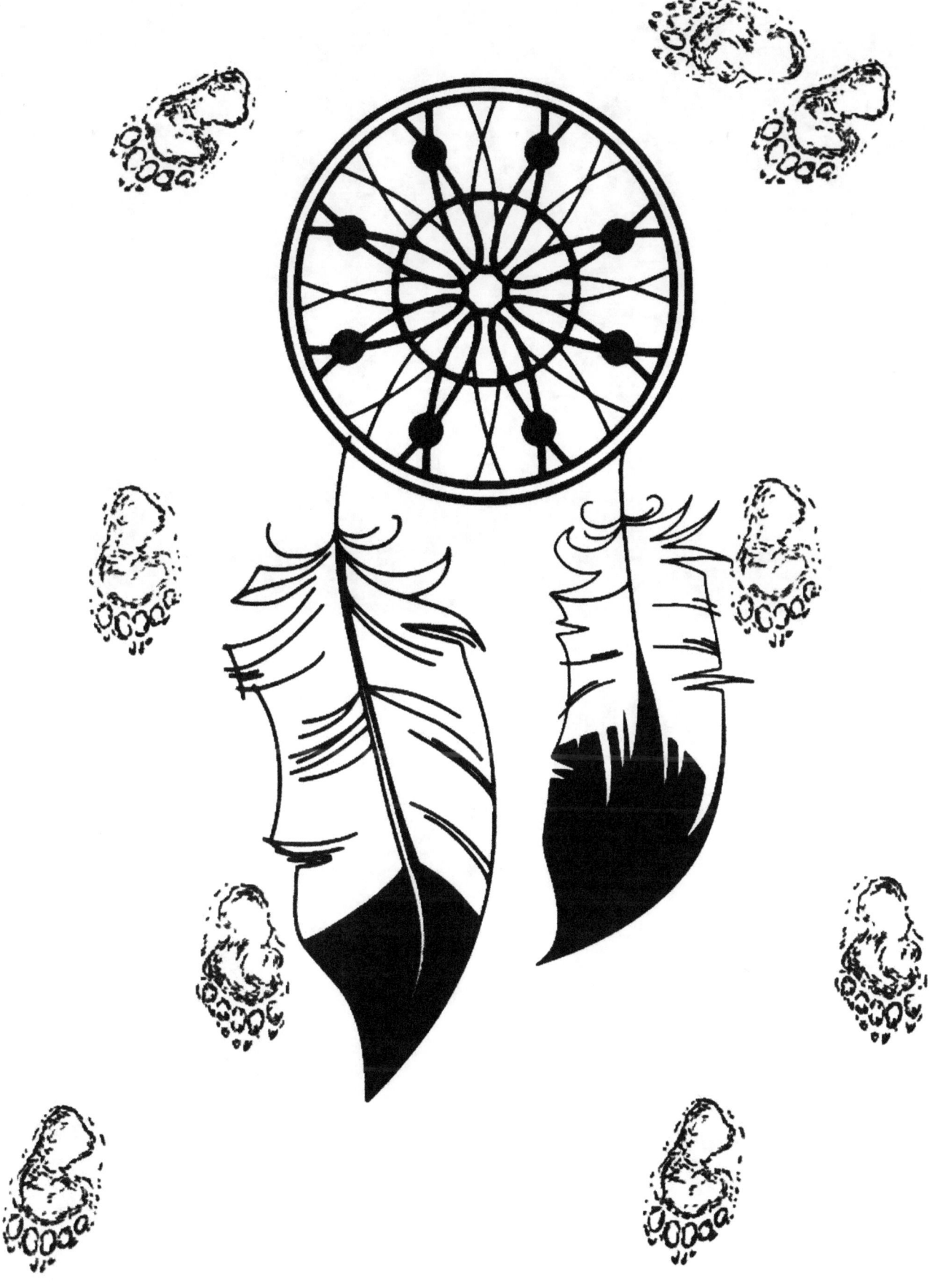

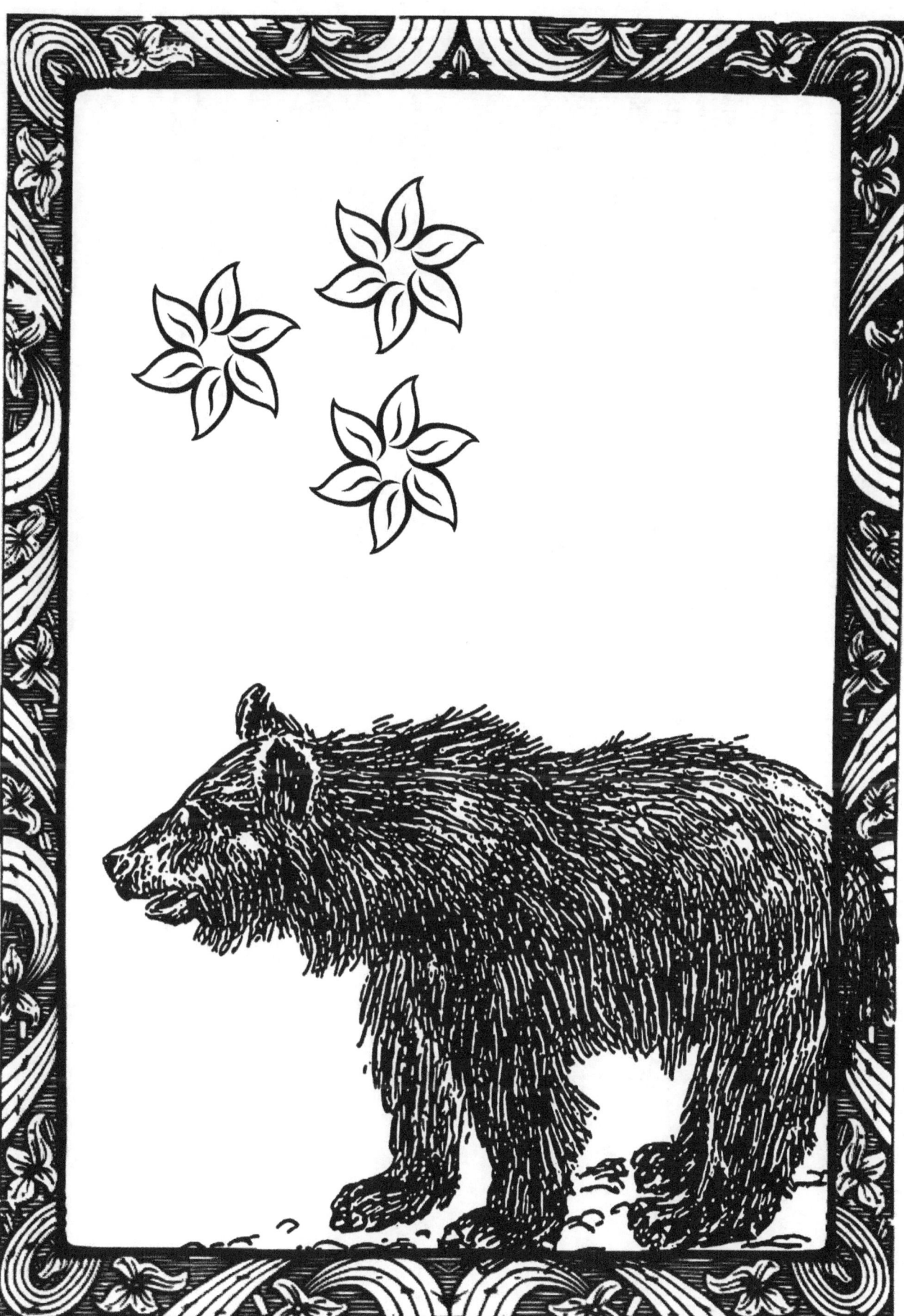

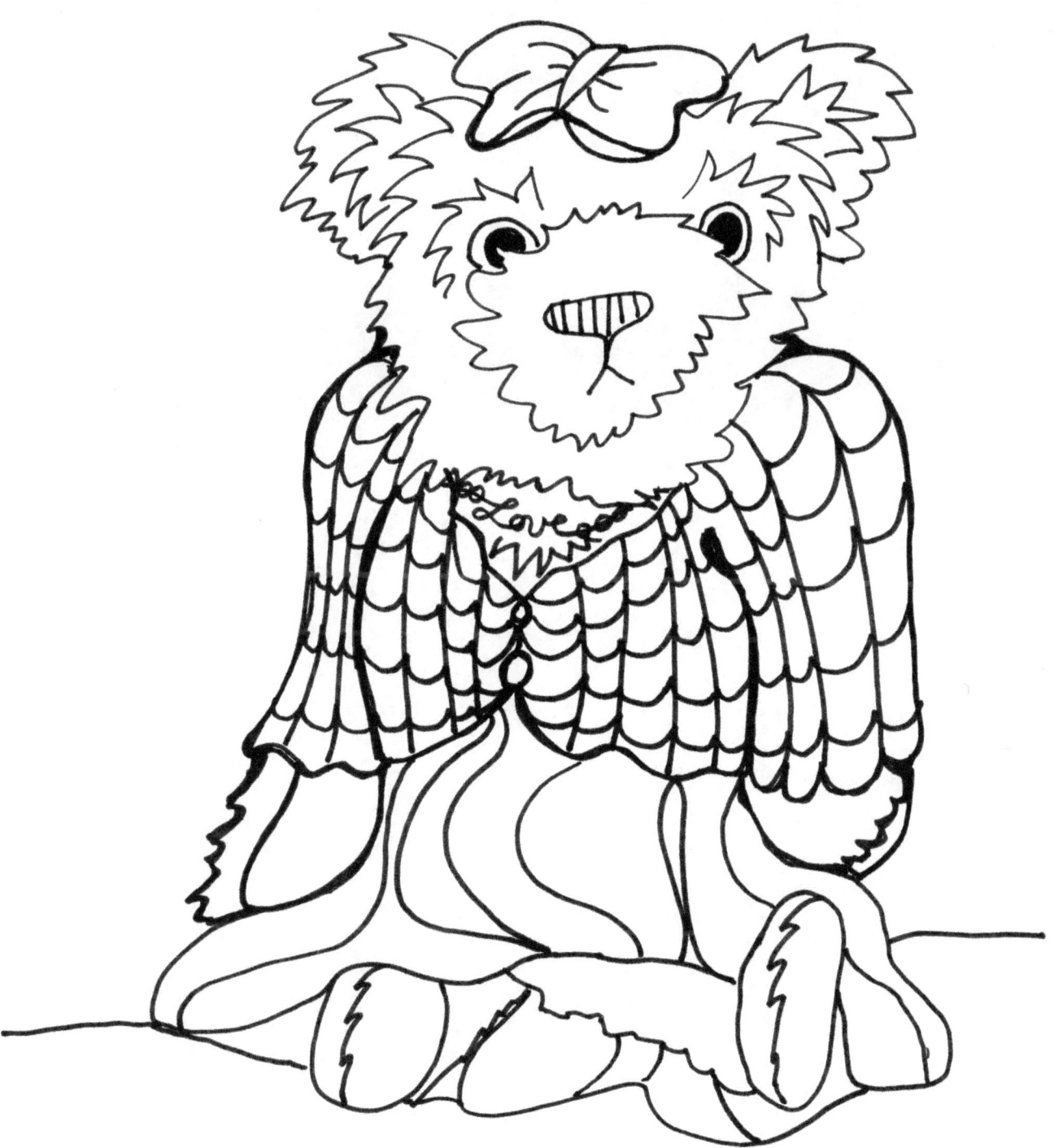

POWERFUL

Brave

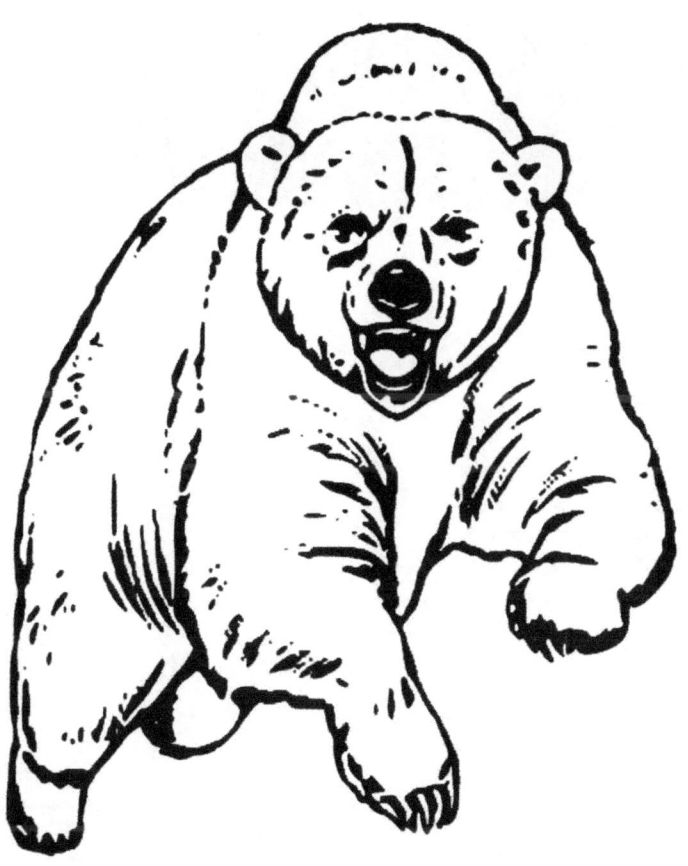

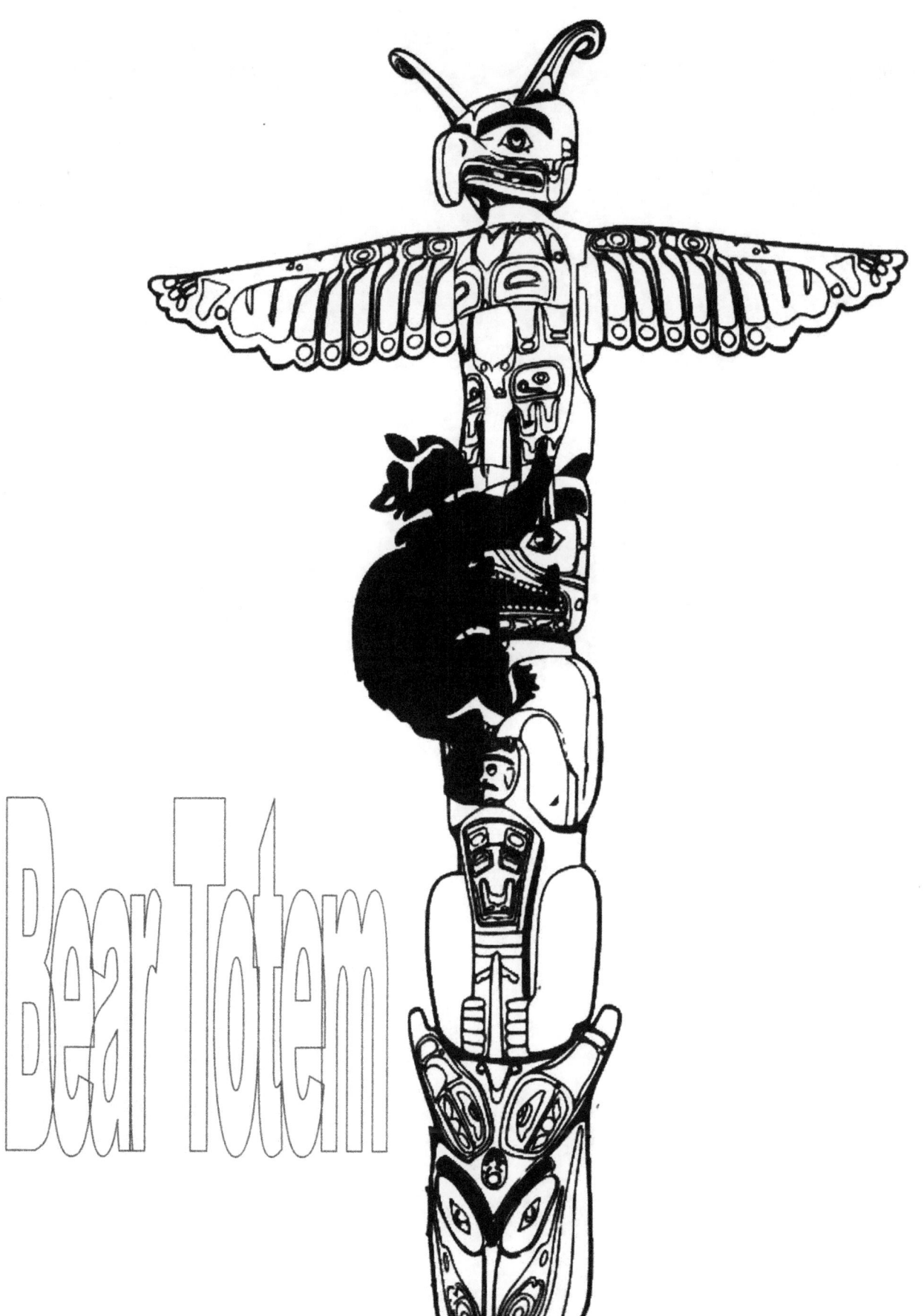

Bear Totem

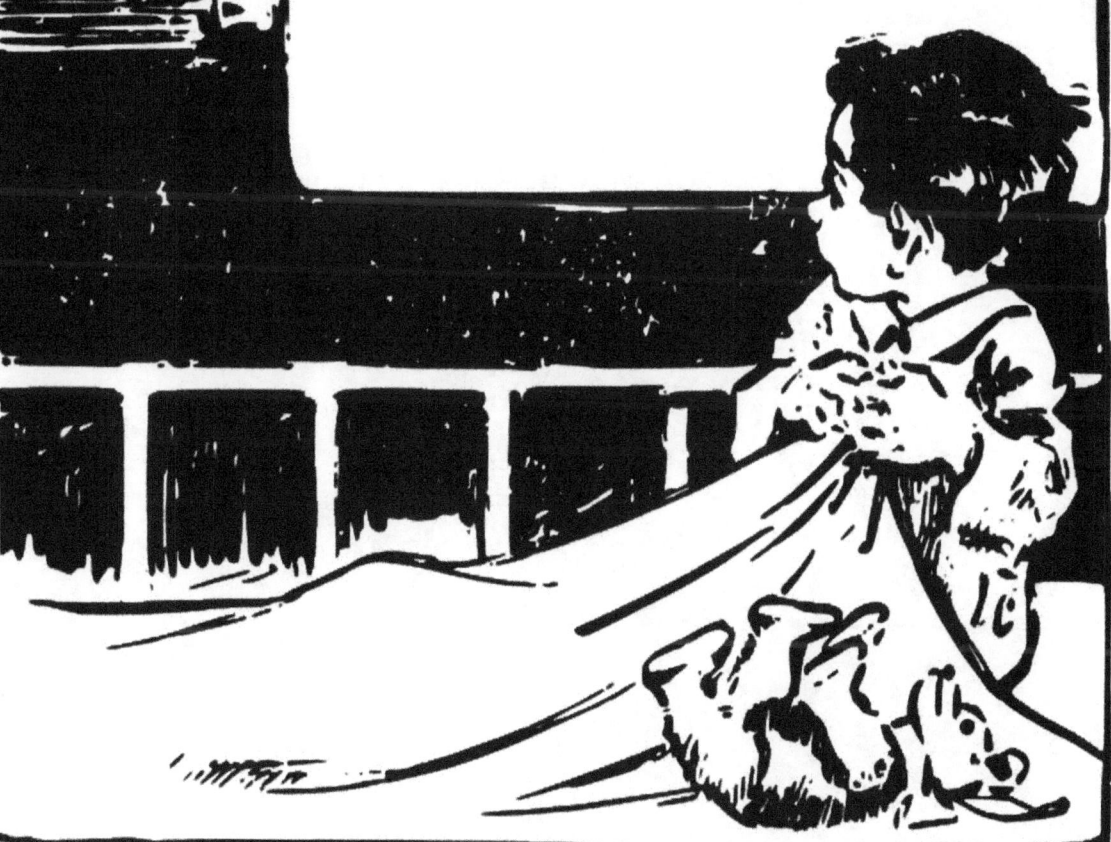

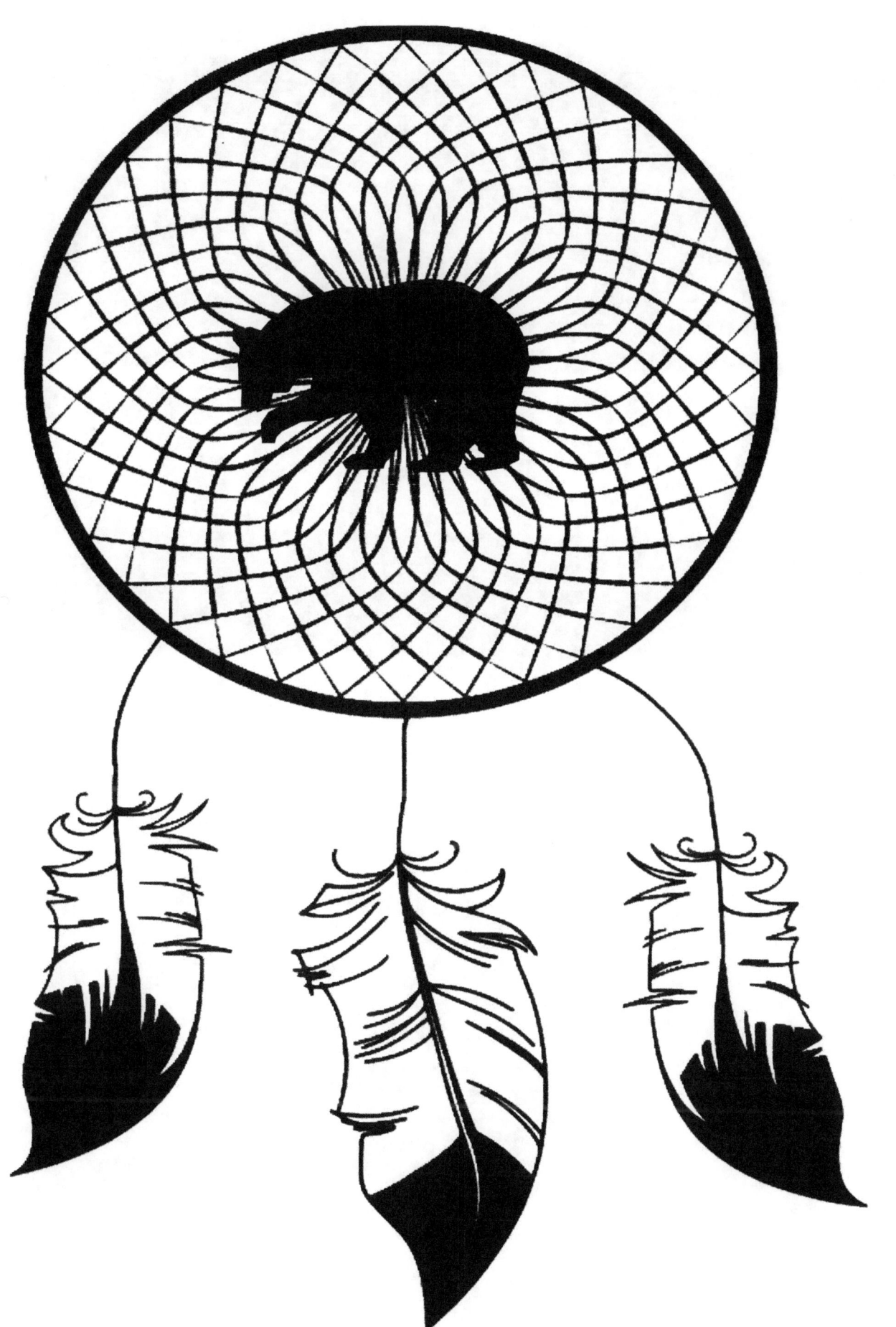

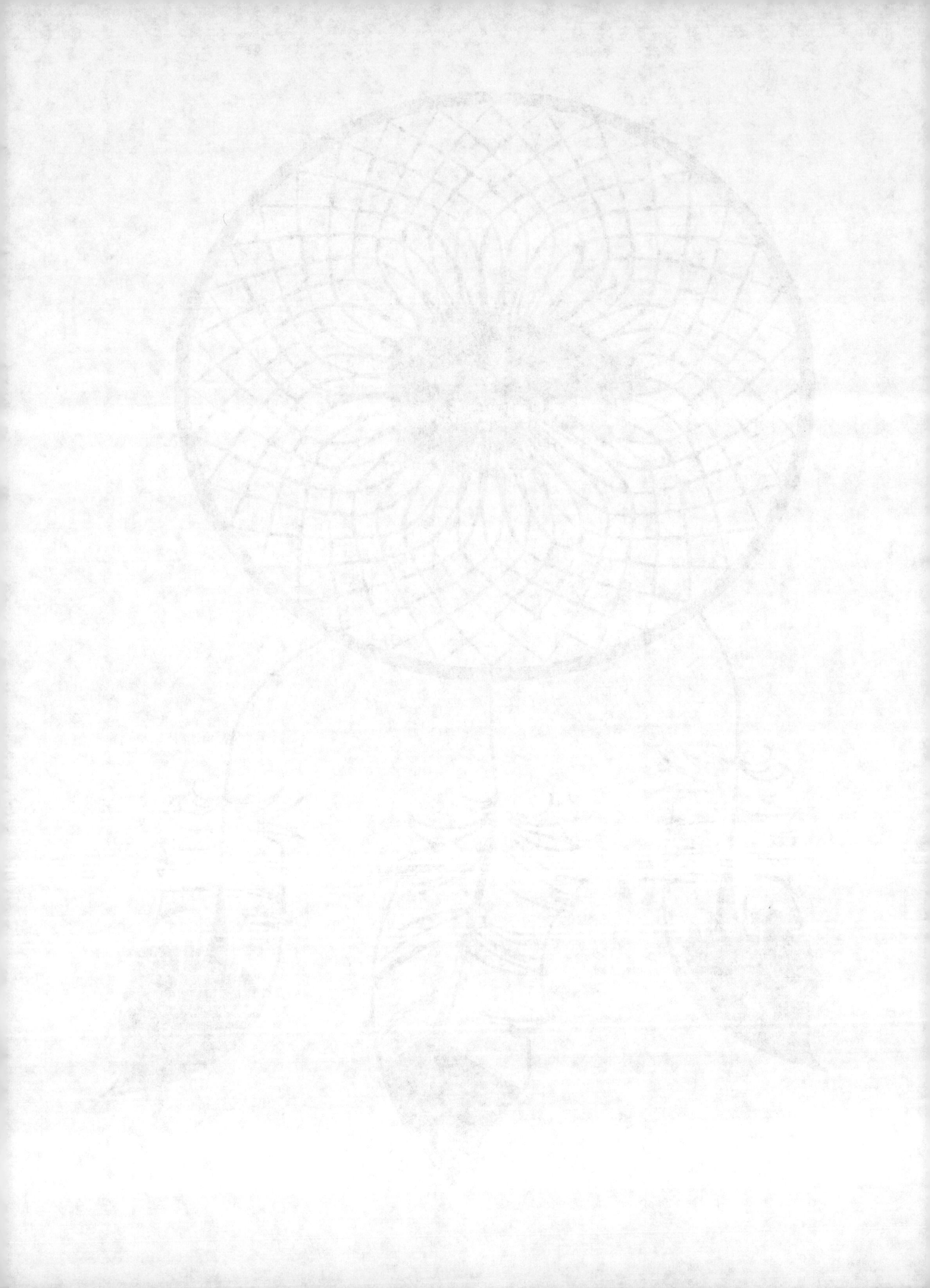

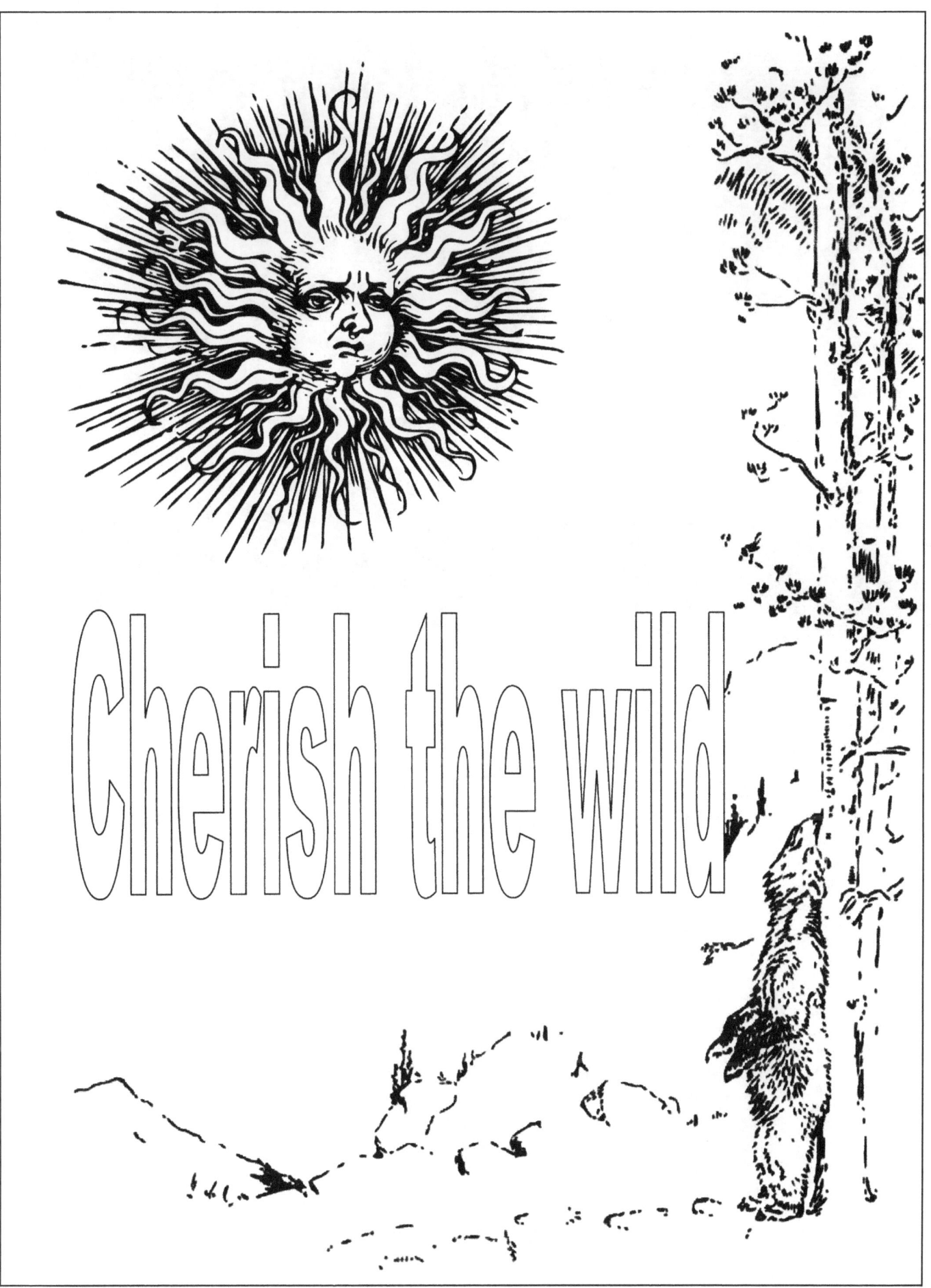

Cherish the wild

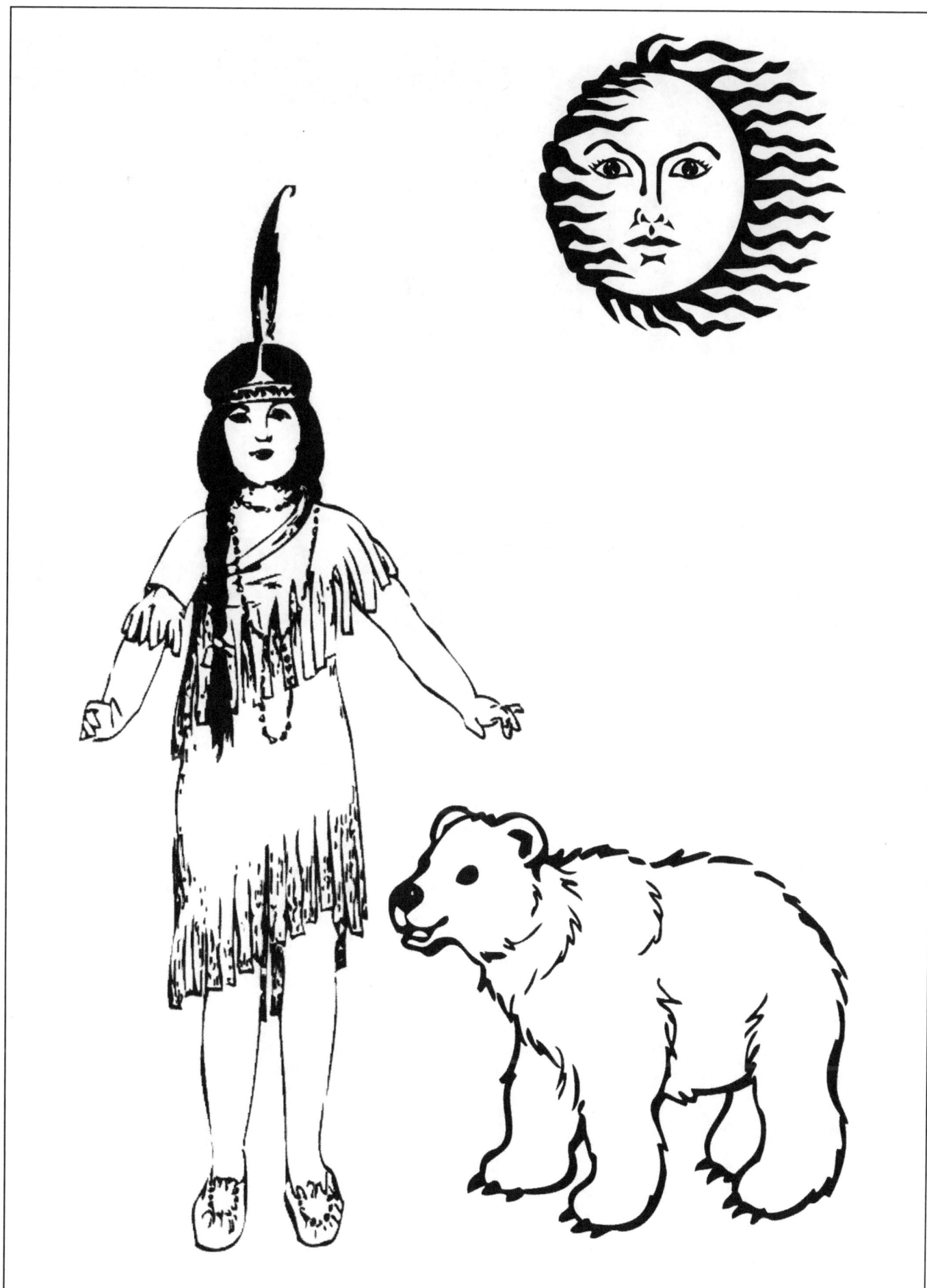

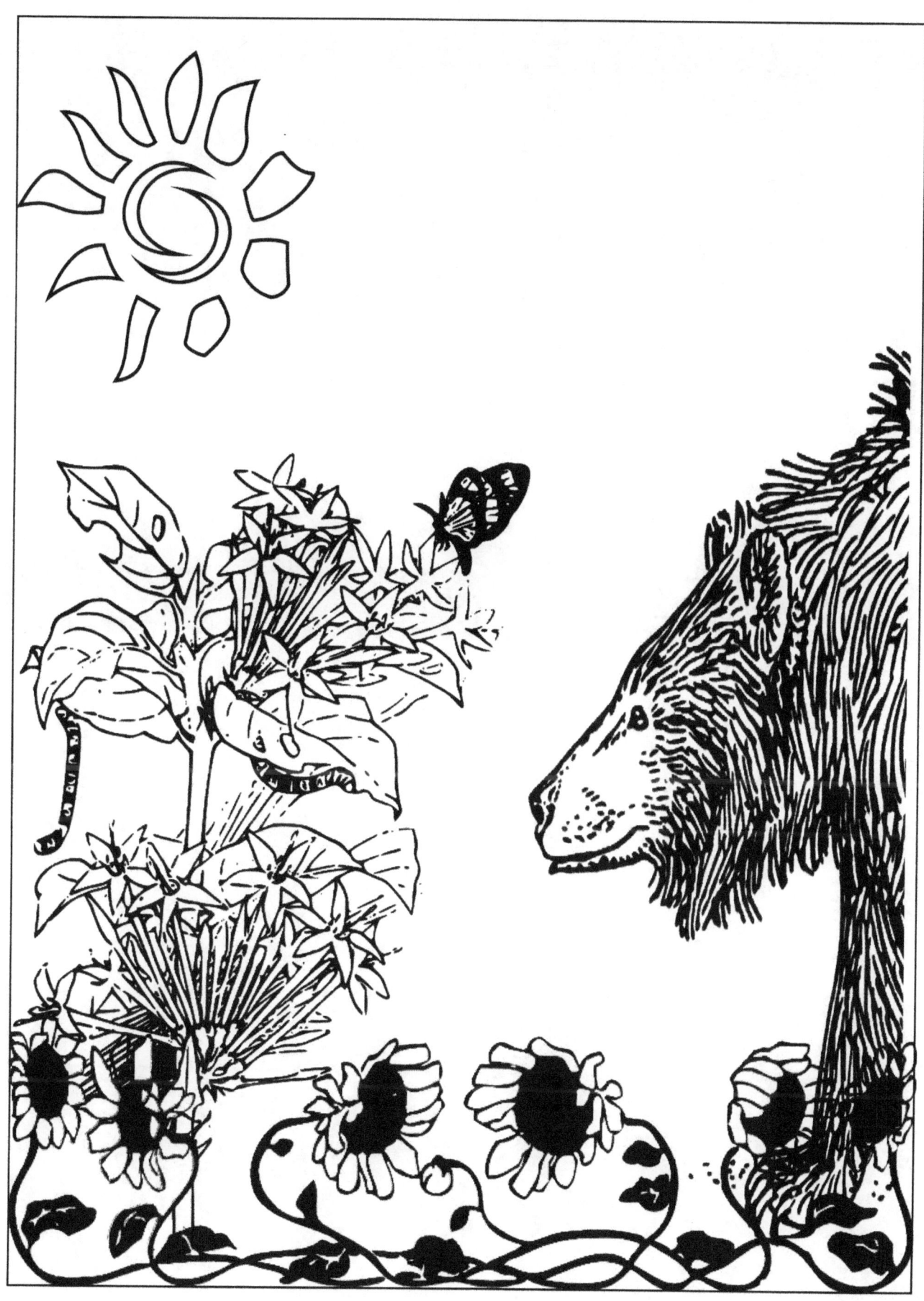

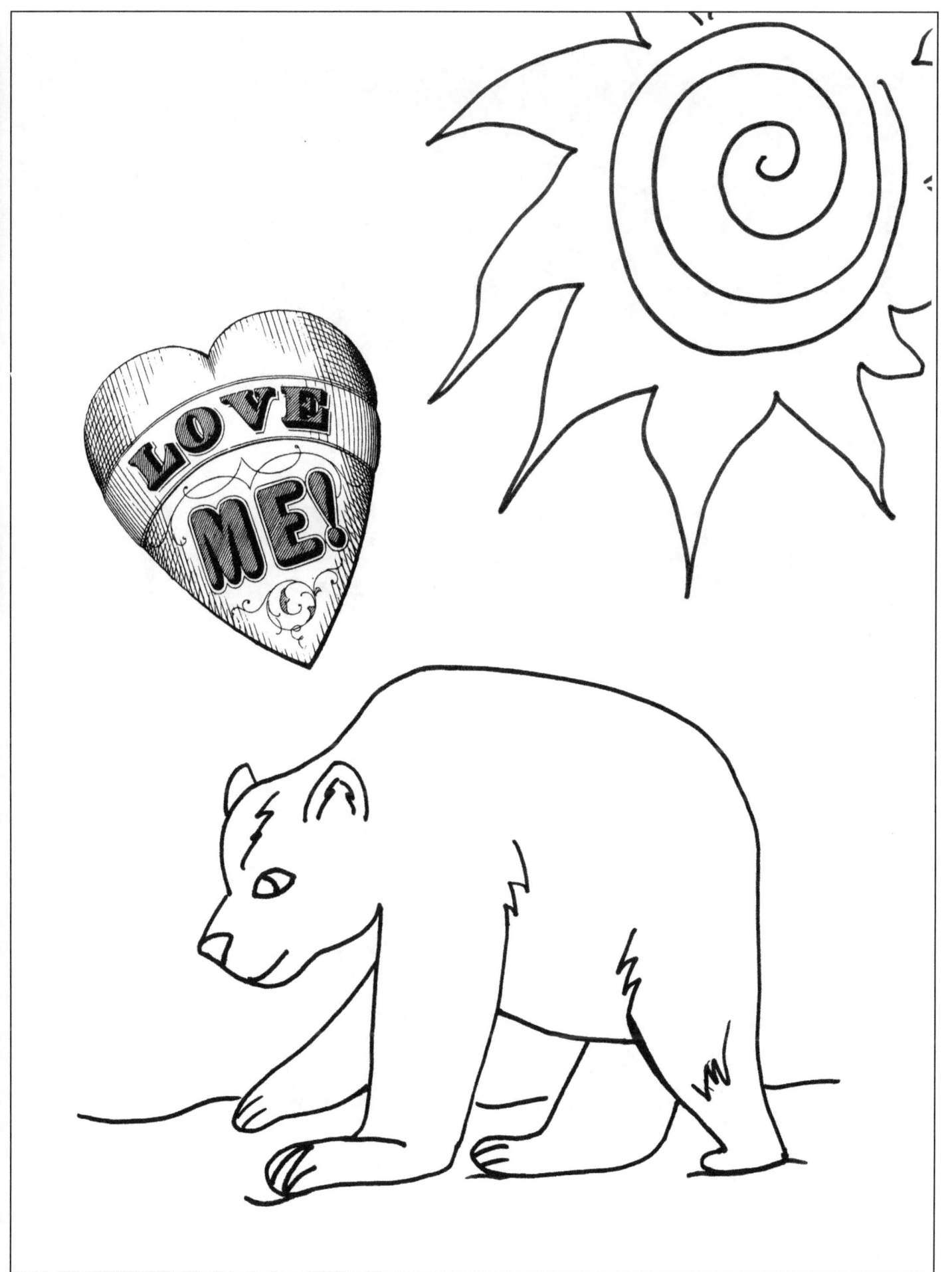

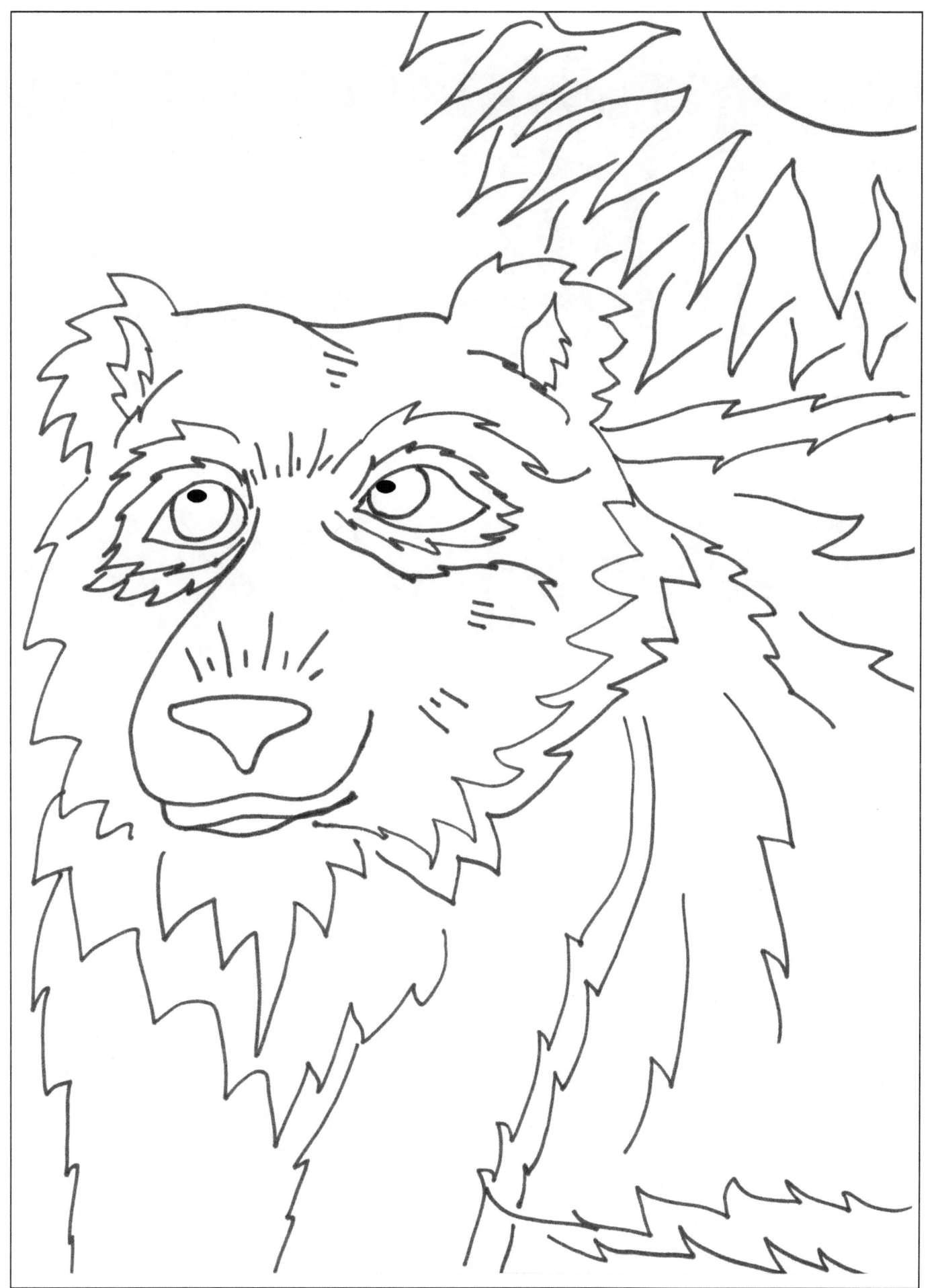

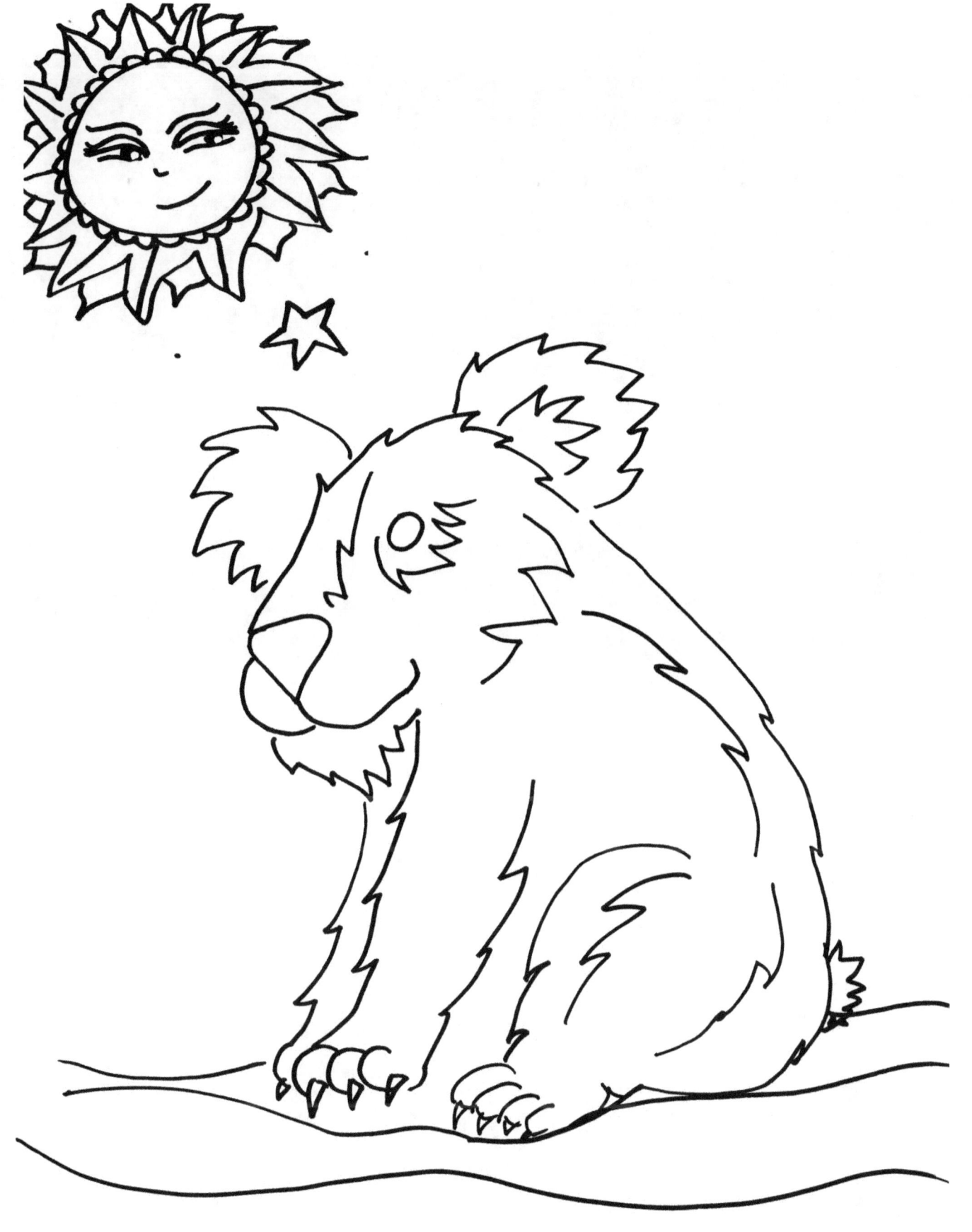

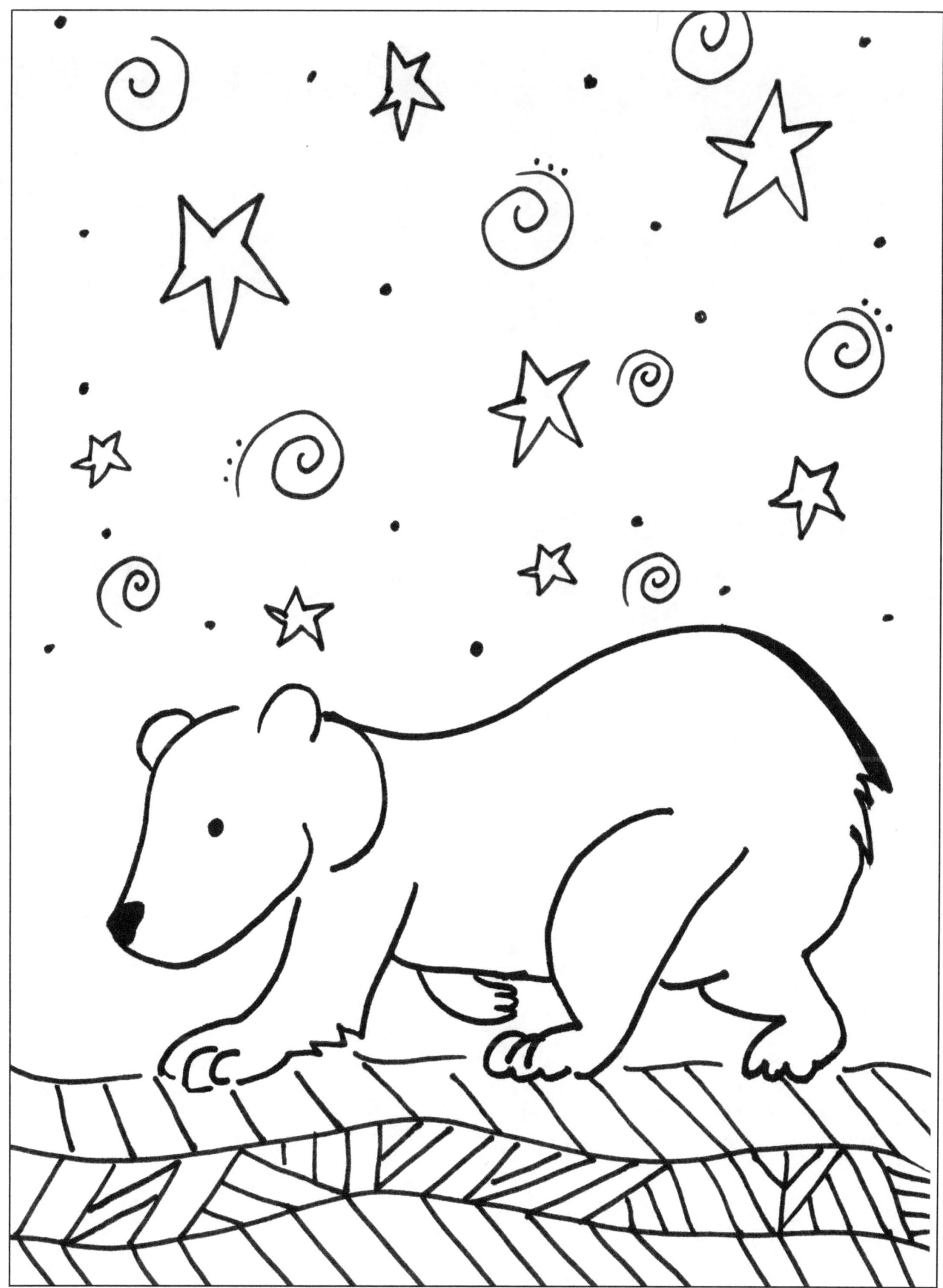

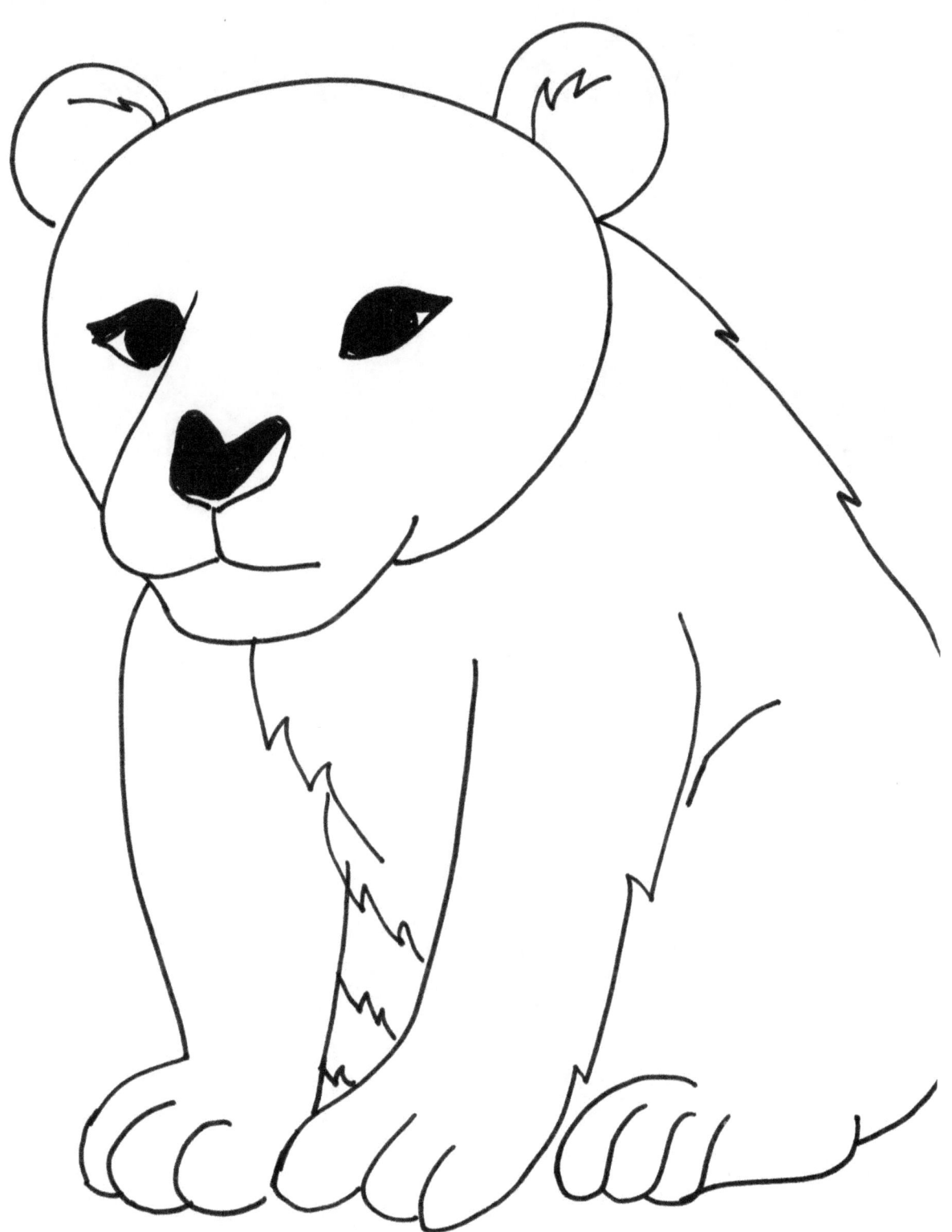

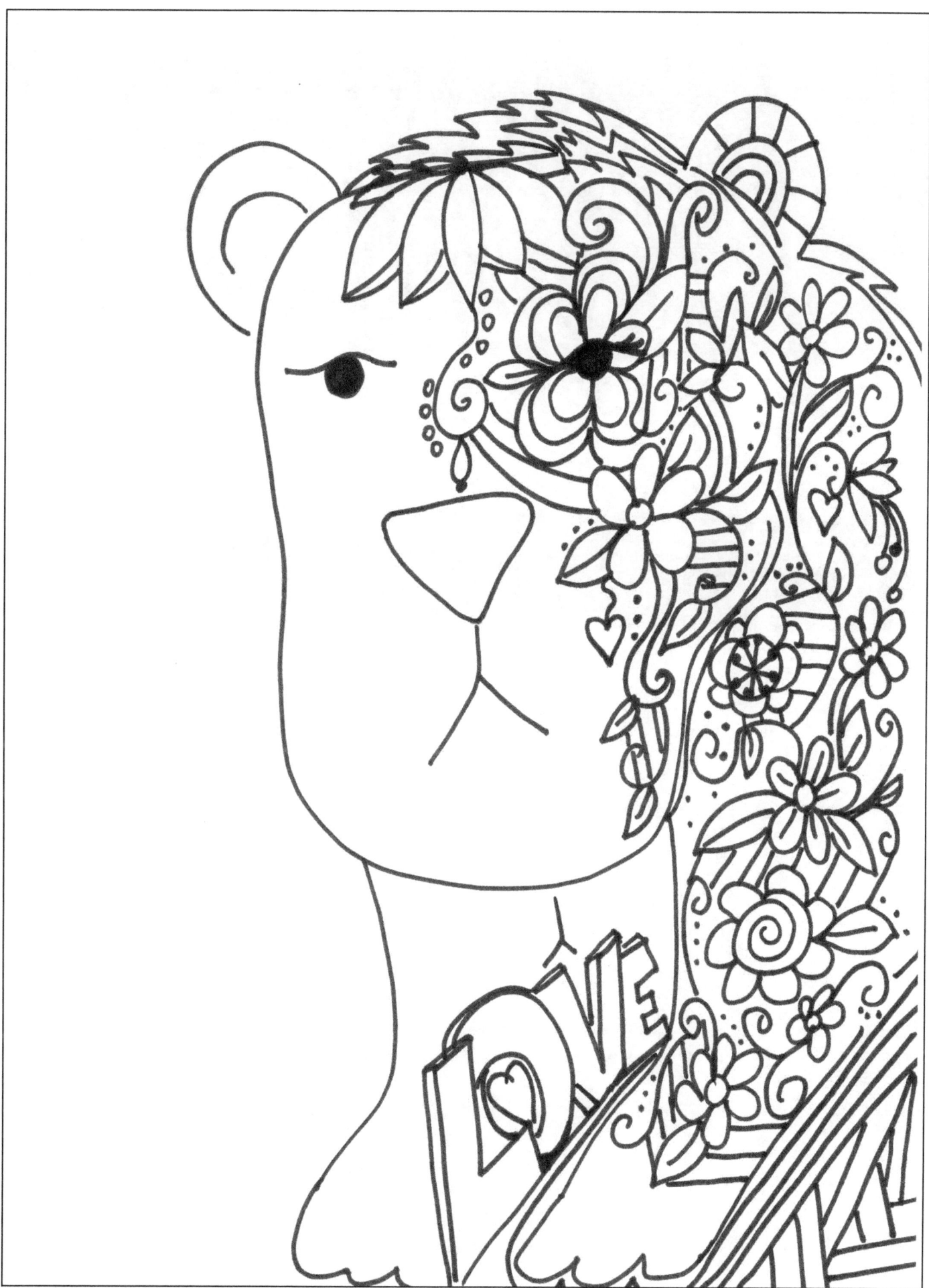

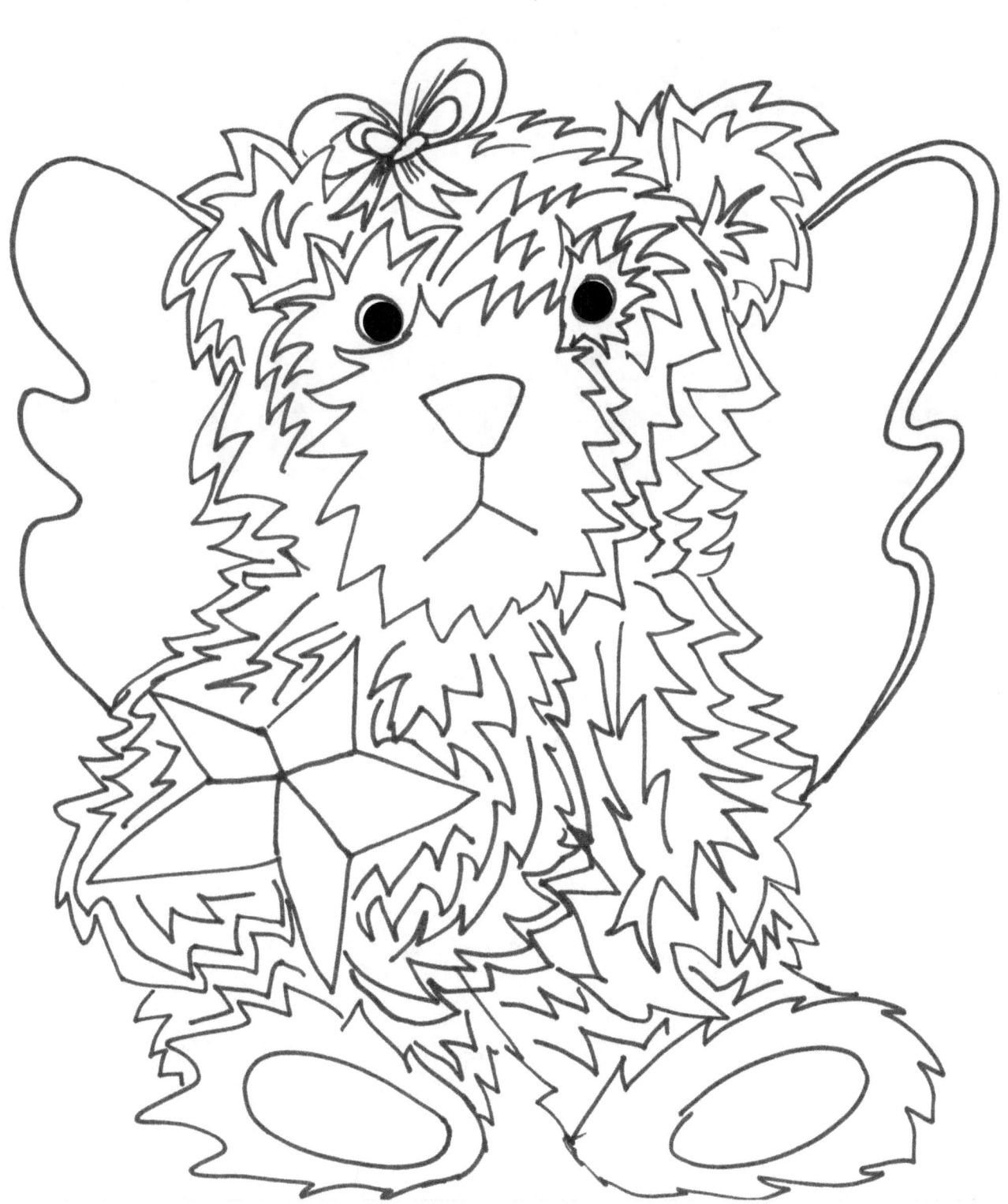

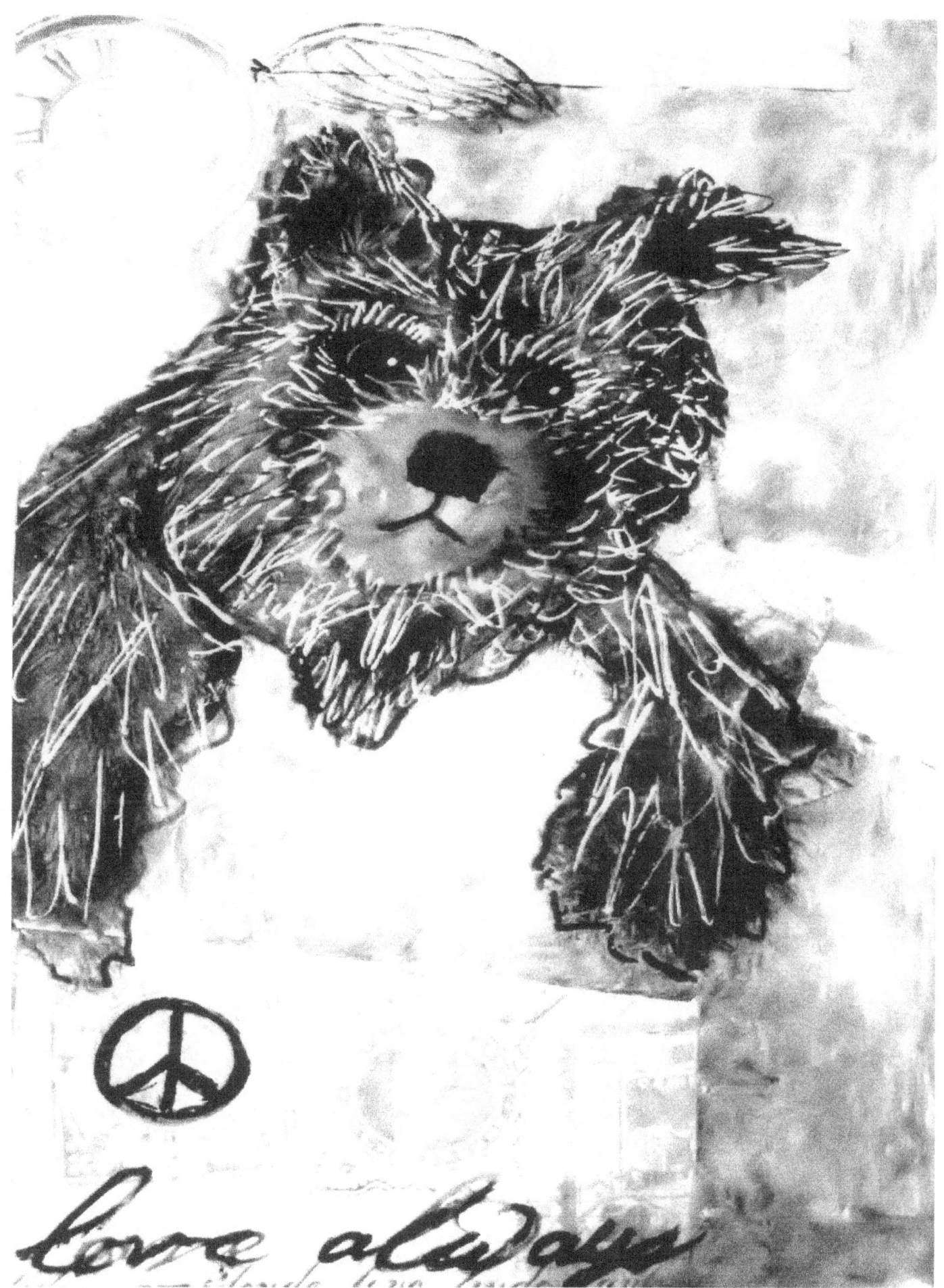

love always

Animal Totem Meditation

You could have someone read this to you slowly, record yourself and play it back or read it through and follow the process. You may choose to lie down or remain seated; whatever you decide allow yourself to be comfortable.

Let's begin to notice the largest sensation of breath in the body.

Allow this breath to expand to include the entire body.

Imagine sending your breath from the top of your head down to the tips of your toes.

Breathe from the top of your head to the knees. Send the breath back to the top of your head.....

Breathe from the top of your head down to your root (the groin area) and back to the top of your head....

Breathe in from the top of your head down to the second chakra, or energy center; located two inches below the belly button and back to the top of your head....

Breathe in from the top of the head down to the third chakra, or energy center; located two inches above the belly button and back to the top of your head....

Next breathe in from the top of the head down to the heart center and back to the top of the head....

Breathe in from the top of the head to the throat center and back to the top of the head....

Breathe in from the top of the head to the third eye point, the area on center of the forehead just above the brow, and back to the top of the head....

Feel the body sinking into a deeper state of relaxation. Allow the body to relax even more......

Relax the scalp and crown of the head…..

Relax your shoulders back and down from the ears……

Relax the upper cheeks, lower cheeks, jaw and tongue. Give the whole face permission to soften……

Relax your ears……

Relax the neck……

Relax the shoulders back and down, if seated, allow the elbows to dangle from the shoulder girdle. If lying down allow the elbows to relax……

Let the hands relax, fingers releasing to their natural curve……

Feel the breath rising and falling in the chest……

Feel the abdomen expand and collapse with the breath……

Let these sensations drop into the back side of the body and release the vertebrae; each one in turn from the cervical spine in the neck all the way down to the sacrum and coccyx……

Allow the hips to relax……

Release any tension in the thighs, your knees, the lower legs, ankles and feet……

Let any remaining tension release from the body from the tips of the toes……

So relaxed from the top of the head all the way down to the tips of the toes……

Any sounds you hear allow you to sink even deeper into a state of rest, of relaxation. As you bring the focus back to the third eye point located on the center of the brow…..

As we begin to take a mental journey.

See, sense, feel or imagine yourself outdoors at your favourite place in nature. A place where you feel content and at peace. The weather is absolutely perfect. The sun is shining. A soft breeze flows against your skin. Birds fly overhead. You can hear the sounds of wildlife surrounding you.

Off to the right you notice a path leading into a forest. Take this path. Notice the texture of the earth beneath your feet. Notice it's consistency; what is the pathway made of? Give it detail. Notice the slight temperature change as you move into the forest.

You can hear the sound of water flowing coming from somewhere up ahead. As you look, some 50 yards ahead of you, you can see a clearing. Walk toward the clearing. As you grow closer still you feel droplets of water upon your face. And you know you have been guided toward a waterfall and a small river flowing from it's base.

As you view the crest of the waterfall you are able to see the sun shining brightly there. Find a place to sit near the waterfall. The surface of the water glitters and sparkles like diamonds. As you get comfortable you hear something off to the right.

You are not afraid…..

You turn to see your Totem Animal coming toward you.

It does not fear you. You smile. And begin to connect to the energy of your beloved Spirit Animal.

It grows closer. You find yourself becoming even more still.

Some six feet away from you the animal stops for a rest. It looks at you with pure trust. And you welcome it into your heart. Slowly you blink your eyes at the being letting it know you too are not a source of fear but rather of universal connection.

The being seems to connect to a part of you so deep and infinite. And you begin to sense it's knowledge. It has secrets to share with you; things you are only now beginning to understand. This is your path, your journey to share the energy of this being.

It looks toward you and then toward the water. And you understand they are here to help you cleanse the body and mind of anything that is no longer serving you.

You carefully step into the warm water feeling the spray of the waterfall on your face.

As you watch the water it turns the most vibrant shade of red.
You allow this colour to fill you, to complete you, to make you whole.

After several minutes you notice the water shifting to a gorgeous shade of orange.
You allow this colour to fill you, to complete you, to make you whole.

After several minutes you notice the water shifting to a wonderful shade of yellow.
You allow this colour to fill you, to complete you, to make you whole.

After several minutes you notice the water shifting to a vibrant shade of green.
You allow this colour to fill you, to complete you, to make you whole.

Your spirit animal watches from a distance. And you know it is helping you to clear your physical body and mind. It supports you.

You look back to the water and notice it shifting in colour again this time to marvelous shade of blue.

You allow this colour to fill you, to complete you, to make you whole.

After several minutes you notice the water shifting now to Indigo; a beautiful mixture of purple-blue similar to a midnight sky.

You allow this colour to fill you, to complete you, to make you whole.

After several minutes you notice the water shifting to a breathtaking purple.

You allow this colour to fill you, to complete you, to make you whole.

From somewhere above you a gorgeous white light shines and begins to bathe your body. From head to toe your entire body begins to glow and you feel complete.

You step out of the water and make your way back to where you were sitting earlier. The sun has warmed the area and it feels so wonderful on your body. You look toward your spirit animal. It is still there watching you. Feel it's love; your connection. The animal begins to share information with you. Information about your current path in life. It tells you what you need to know in this moment.

You may hear words, see images, feel an attachment to them or connect to an inner sense of knowing. Listen to what they have to share...... (3-5 minutes of silence)

Now take the time to ask any questions you may have for clarification or to receive further understanding...(3-5 minutes of silence)

Thank the animal for sharing space with you. And return to the awareness to the present moment; knowing you can find your spirit animal whenever you choose as they are deeply connected with your heart.

About the Creator:

Tammy Lawrence-Cymbalisty is an Alternative Care provider working in the Kitchener/Waterloo Region. Since 2001 she has helped many people find peace, happiness, harmony and further purpose in their lives.

Tammy holds many degrees including: B.A. Sociology (Trent University), Certified Yoga Teacher, Reiki Master/Teacher, HypnoBirthing® Practitioner, Meditation Teacher, Workshop facilitator, Writer, Personal Growth Coach.

She lives with her husband, two felines and a school of fins in Cambridge, ON

Find out more by following Tammy on social media:

http://www.twitter.com/tllc

http://www.tinyurl.com/tlcservices

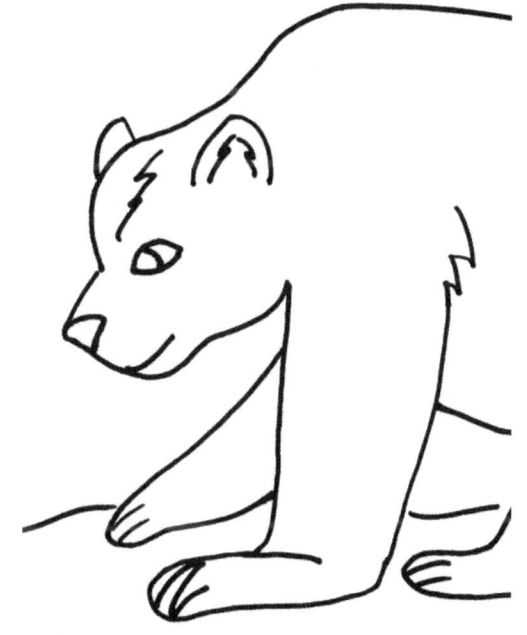

May you find peace

May you find happiness

May you be free from suffering

Namaste, Tammy

www.ingramcontent.com/pod-product-compliance
Lightning Source LLC
Chambersburg PA
CBHW080725190526
45169CB00006B/2518